ABOUT THIS BOOK

Easing Life's Hurts compassionately encourages readers to choose a biblical perspective toward facing life's bumps, bruises, and disappointments. While optimistic, it makes no claim that all life's hurts can be blocked. Unavoidable hits and losses help us grasp our common humanity. Neither can all pains be erased; some of them stay with us as crucial and challenging aspects of our new reality. They shape our souls toward wisdom, kindness, and understanding.

Wilhelm and Bagents remind us that we're not alone in facing setbacks. They also remind us that we're never powerless victims. When we hurt, we can choose to seek God's help and welcome His grace. As we heal—often even as part of our healing—we find allies whom we come to identify as gifts from God. We discover strengths, many available for immediate access, some awaiting development, and others new to the moment. And we come to welcome the soothing power of humor.

As we hurt, we find God lovingly ready to comfort and assist. As He eases our hurts, He also gently pulls us to use what we experience—what we have learned, are learning, and will learn—to help ease the hurts of others.

ABOUT THE AUTHORS

Jack P. Wilhelm (PhD, Auburn University) was a minister, educator, and author. He began preaching at the age of fifteen and served various congregations in Alabama and Tennessee as minister for over sixty years. Wilhelm was president of Mars Hill Bible School in Florence, Alabama from 1962–1983 and 2000. With his wife Mary Alice, he published over twenty books for personal and class studies.

Bill Bagents (DMin, Amridge University) is Professor of Ministry, Counseling, and Biblical Studies at Heritage Christian University in Florence, Alabama.

EASING LIFE'S HURTS

JACK P. WILHELM
BILL BAGENTS

Foreword by
RICKEY COLLUM

CYPRESS
PUBLICATIONS

Copyright© 2001 by Jack P. Wilhelm

Second edition published by Cypress Publications 2020

Manufactured in the United States

Cataloging-in-Publication Data

Wilhelm, Jack (Jack Petty), 1930–2016

Easing life's hurts / by Jack P. Wilhelm and Bill Bagents

2nd ed.

p. cm.

Includes Scripture index.

ISBN 978-1-7347665-1-6 (pbk,); 978-1-7347665-3-0 (ebook)

1. Christian life. 2. Psychology—Biblical teaching. 3. Personality—Biblical teaching. I. Author. II. Bagents, William Ronald, 1956-. III. Title.

158.1—dc20 Library of Congress Control Number: 2020941152

Cover design by Brad McKinnon and Brittany Vander Maas.

All rights reserved. No part of this publication may be reproduced, distributed, stored in a retrieval system, or transmitted in any form by any means without the prior written permission of the publisher, except in the case of brief quotations embodies in critical reviews and certain other noncommercial uses permitted by copyright law.

The Bible version used in this publication is THE NEW KING JAMES VERSION, Copyright © 1979, 1980, 1982, Thomas Nelson, Inc. Publishers. Use by permission. All rights reserved.

Cypress Publications
3625 Helton Drive
PO Box HCU
Florence, AL 35630
www.hcu.edu

CONTENTS

Appreciation	xi
Foreword	xiii
1. "Ugly Duckling" Issues: Acceptance or Rejection	1
2. The Power of a Biblical Self-Image	15
3. The Critic's Sting and the Gossip's Gore	26
4. When Good Words Don't Come	40
5. The Love Traps	50
6. The Limits of Love	69
7. The Hurts Caused by Others	81
8. Forgiveness	95
9. Martial Arts and Marital Hurts	106
10. Marital Stress	121
11. Child Rearing Hurts	133
12. Parenting Pains	149
13. Hurts Caused by Things	161
14. Our Attitude Toward Money	174
15. Career Jolts	185
16. When Hurts Shall Be No More	196
Scripture Index	215

To the Memory of
John A. Wilhelm (1894-1972)
and
Octie Petty Wilhelm (1898-1952)

My parents who did their best while coping with economic and health struggles to provide a foundation for a successful life and memories of a good home.

Jack P. Wilhelm

In Honor of
Ed and Sue Bagents
with love

An old Irish proverb reads, "It is in the shelter of each other that the people live."

By your example, your teaching, and your love, you have sheltered me from so many of life's hurts. Everything good has been easier because of you.

Bill Bagents

Appreciation

During nearly 60 years of ministry, I have had the privilege of being a co-worker with many ministers. Not one has been more pleasant and cooperative than Bill Bagents. We both appreciate the great encouragement the Mars Hill church at Florence, Alabama, gives us. This book is the product of classes we taught from January to May, 2001, on alternate Monday nights to over three dozen different souls who requested enrichment studies. You will need to look up the scripture references for maximum benefit. My special thanks to my wife, Mary Alice, for checking every reference to assure accuracy.

The theme for these studies, "Easing Life's Hurts," was chosen primarily because it has an application sooner or later to everybody. We all experience hurts in life. If one set of them is eased, another volley from a different direction replaces them.

Some years ago, one of my other co-workers, Edsel Burleson, said that when Christians have problems, "All is not gloom and defeat, however, because Christians know there is hope." He quoted Romans 5:3–4: "We glory in tribulations also: knowing that tribulation works perseverance; and perseverance, experience; and experience, hope." He also quoted Charles Spurgeon who said, "Stars may be seen from the bottom of a deep well, when they cannot be seen from the top of the mountain. So many things are learned in adversity which the prosperous man dreams not of."

Bill Bagents and I send these lessons forth in the hope that some of your hurts in life will be eased by these time-tested thoughts that have helped us and others in the past.

Jack P. Wilhelm
Summer, 2001

Second Edition Appreciation

Jack Wilhelm always treated me better than I deserved. I miss the wisdom of his funny and insightful sayings. Among my favorites: "Preachers make their living by the sweat of their tongues" and "He couldn't help it; he was just being himself." Jack did more to help others, bless the church, and further Christian education than any of us know. And he loved doing it God's way (Matthew 6:1–4).

Jack's kindness continues through his family, who graciously granted Cypress Publications permission to issue this second edition of the book.

We also appreciate the team of editors and friends who designed a new cover, created a scripture index, and made other improvements. Special thanks to Laura Bagents, Brad McKinnon, and Jamie Cox. BIG APPRECIATION to Rickey Collum for the most generous foreword.

Bill Bagents
Summer, 2020

FOREWORD

During these days and in this present world, we need help "easing life's hurts." Everyone hurts. We all have times of struggle. The Bible states that we should "Bear one another's burdens." When I encountered troubles in my life, I was blessed enough to have access to some of the best counsel. Dr. Jack Wilhelm and Dr. Bill Bagents were my "go to guys." I have had the privilege to study under both of these faithful and caring men, and I am better for it. This book is a compilation of the works of both of my friends—and is an excellent book for those who struggle or those who want to help those who struggle.

Jack Wilhelm began the daily TV program "Televisit with the Bible" in 1957 and was a principal speaker for a period that spanned 50 years. Dr. Wilhelm served 22 years as president of Mars Hill Bible School (1962–1983 and 2000). He served on the Mars Hill Bible School Board of Directors from 1997–2000 and for two years as

FOREWORD

an administrator at Knoxville Christian School (1983–1985). From 1980–1992 he published the RSVP Newsletter for ministers in all 50 states. Jack and his wife, Mary Alice, have published over 20 books for personal and class studies.

Jack Wilhelm was my mentor. Between the first and second editions of this book, I had the solemn honor of preaching the funeral of my good friend and mentor. I would not be a preacher if it were not for Jack. His help and encouragement was the solid rock I clung to in my early years preaching. His loving heart and biblical wisdom are missed daily.

Bill Bagents serves as Professor of Ministry, Counseling, and Biblical Studies at Heritage Christian University. He teaches graduate courses in ministry and undergraduate courses in Old Testament, New Testament, ministry, counseling, and church leadership. He served as an elder and associate minister with the Mars Hill Church of Christ in Florence. Bill was a co-founder and counselor with the Alpha Center, a Christian counseling center. He has worked numerous years in individual and marital/family counseling.

Bill is also involved in numerous mission works. He has taught in South Africa, Namibia, Albania and Jamaica. He has been a guest lecturer in Nigerian Christian Bible College and West Nigeria Christian College. And he participated in the Palliative Care Chaplaincy with the local hospital.

I first met Bill and his wife, Laura, while he was youth director and associate preacher at Florence Boulevard Church of Christ in the late 1980s. I have had the

FOREWORD

privilege of working for and with this fine Christian man ever since. His love for the Lord and his love for the lost are exemplary. I have had the honor of working beside Bill and Laura on mission trips and consider them both to be dear friends.

It is clear that I have a love for both of the writers of this book, but I also believe in this effort they have published. It is a biblical way to look at the everyday problems that we encounter and how to overcome those struggles.

Rickey Collum
Hackleburg, Alabama
January 2020

EASING LIFE'S HURTS

"UGLY DUCKLING" ISSUES: ACCEPTANCE OR REJECTION

JACK P. WILHELM

Little babies come into this world making their presence known by demanding acceptance and attention. That is normal. It is also desirable that they find acceptance because they are a "heritage from the Lord" (Psalm 127:3).

Unfortunately, there have been times when little ones were not well-received and have not gotten a fair shake. The pagan world sometimes treated little ones very brutally. A child might be presented to a father who would not acknowledge it as his child. Apparently human sacrifices of children were made to Molech (See Leviticus 20:1–6). And there was the time when Herod had all the babies under age two killed in his vain attempt to kill the Christ child. Even in our civilized age, we are appalled to know that little female babies are not welcomed in the world's most populated country. Emotional trauma about acceptance and rejection have scarred many babies since the world began.

"UGLY DUCKLING" ISSUES

EARLY STRUGGLES FOR ACCEPTANCE

The scars of rejection dot the landscape of Biblical history. Abraham's family history is a case in point—and the world is paying a price for it even in this twenty-first century. Read Genesis 21. You will see the sad story of how Hagar and her son Ishmael were sent away because of the inner conflict Sarah felt when she assumed that her son Isaac's future was threatened. When you see a story on the world news tonight of a Palestinian youth throwing rocks at Israeli youth and policemen, you will be reminded of how long lasting the hurts of rejection are.

In Bible classes, our children sing, "Oh, once there were three wandering Jews." Abraham, Isaac and Jacob and their families meandered over the hills of Palestine for years, seeking acceptance. Typical of their struggles was Isaac's search for water. He had to re-dig the wells his father had dug years before, only to have them filled again by enemies who did not want either generation as neighbors. Finally, Isaac dug a well and called it Rehoboth, because, "Now the Lord has made room for us, and we shall be fruitful in the land" (Genesis 26:22).

When Jesus was born, "he came to his own and his own received him not" (John 1:11). We are thankful that Christ came and showed the world how to find peace and acceptance. Even as he did so, he himself was "despised and rejected by men, a man of sorrows and acquainted with grief" (Isaiah 53:3).

CHILDHOOD EXPERIENCES THAT HURT

Some of you who are reading this can recall vividly some of the experiences you had as children that hurt. Hopefully, the hurts have been assuaged with the passing of time, but for many, deeply embedded scars may remain. It may have been that you were made to feel as if you were the "ugly duckling" in your family. The popularity of the Cinderella story may be rooted in the fact that her story seemed all too real to some, except that the handsome young prince never did show up!

Hans Christian Andersen wrote children's stories but was not a happy youth. His family was poor; his father died insane. He wanted to be an actor but was told that he was too ugly.

He tried to write but was rebuked for producing inferior drivel. He received little praise. In his diary, he once wrote, "Blame dulls me; praise gives me courage." We wonder what he might have been able to achieve had he been popularly accepted.

The story of Joseph who was literally hated and mistreated by his brothers who resented the partiality he received from their father is a classic of cruel sibling rivalry (Genesis 37). Or perhaps you received numerous "put downs" and very little praise as a child, all of which left any self-esteem you had in a shambles. Or maybe there was a "pecking order" in which you felt victimized by the class bully. Maybe you felt that the teachers had "pets" who could do no wrong, while you were convinced that they picked on you. My years as a teacher and administrator, however, prompt me to say that there may well be another side to this. I have seen too many good teachers victimized unfairly by lazy students and gullible parents.

I recall a statement Rufus Hibbett, a prominent educator, made once: "No teacher is going to be mean to a good student." There could be an exception, but generally that is true. Good teachers may well be slandered because they have more interest in wanting students to succeed in life than the students and their parents do. A lot of good teachers have lived long enough to have former students seek them out in later life to thank them for "picking on them."

PHYSICAL FACTORS THAT HAVE POTENTIAL TO HURT

The world has said that if you want to be somebody, you have to be beautiful or handsome, clever and smart, healthy and wealthy, and agile and athletic. Most of us reply in return that we are left out because we are ugly, dumb, poor, and clumsy. If that were literally true on all counts, we might really feel hurt, but we tend to exaggerate our deficiencies—influenced no doubt by all the TV celebrities and advertising we are exposed to.

At the same time, there are some extremes where physical situations do have a bearing on acceptance or rejection. Remember the hunchback of Notre Dame? The "Quasimodo" factor is a reminder that some people do have grotesque deformities that serve as obstacles. We should be grateful that great advances in cosmetic surgery have blessed many. We have all read with pleasure about doctors and nurses who have traveled to undeveloped countries and done re-constructive surgery that changed the lives of many. Our society sometimes exaggerates size and appearance. At times we think the world is making some headway to put a premium on what a person knows and what he thinks more than on mere appearance, and then something will happen to remind us that we still have a long way to go to make permanent headway.

There's a story about the eminent judge Oliver Wendell Holmes that should teach us something. The judge, who was rather small in stature, was once in the company of friends who were not only larger than he but more outspoken. One of them said, "Judge, I guess it makes you feel a little awkward to be so small and in the company of us big fellows."

Judge Holmes replied, "Yes, it makes me feel like a dime in the midst of a bunch of pennies."

It's interesting to note that by the time a successor was chosen to replace King Saul, God told Samuel not to use the same superficial criteria about physical stature that had been used for Saul's selection. He said, "The Lord does not see as man sees; for man looks at the outward appearance, but the Lord looks at the heart!" (1 Samuel 16:7)

SPECIAL CHILDREN

Physically speaking, there are differences at times that mark some children as "special" who will need a lot of extra care and understanding, especially from their

"UGLY DUCKLING" ISSUES

parents. At times I think of these parents as the real heroes in life. We might say that God really honored them by feeling that he could depend on them to provide love and care to children with special needs who might not have gotten such loving care from anyone else. Knowing that does not lessen the fatigue and exhaustion they feel, but it may give them the heart to go on. The greatest hurt these parents feel may be the reaction of insensitive peers who hold their little ones at arm's length because they are "different."

There is the child with Down's Syndrome. The development stages of these children will be slower. Acceptance is a major factor in their well-being, determined in part by whether caregivers have the love and patience that are necessary to care for them. We all know children with Down syndrome who are especially sweet and regarded as blessings by their parents. There is a good bit of material on the internet that will help caretakers of children with Down syndrome.

There is also the autistic child. Small children under age 3 who are afflicted in this way are often very unresponsive to human contact, even seeming to lack attachment to parents. If you will do a search on the net using the keyword Autism, you should be able to find helpful information.

There is also the Epileptic child, as well as children who have various learning disabilities and some with mixed racial backgrounds. These will sometimes be the focus of extra attention as they go through their school years. The reaction of their peers can at times cause hurts, but you will also be greatly surprised at times at the extra care and acceptance that some of their classmates give them, depending on their local school climate. In the days before civil rights were more clearly defined by law, my wife was once the sponsor of a ninth-grade class that, on their own, cancelled a class event when they learned that one of their class members was excluded. Needless to say, the role of parents and teachers is pivotal in helping children have self-esteem.

Children with a high measure of self-esteem have fewer hurts in life. One of the best ways to build self-esteem in children is to listen to them. You do not have to let them rule the roost, but you can provide the climate where they know they are a part of the family and are loved.

SOCIAL FACTORS THAT CAUSE REJECTION

There are many cultural differences and behaviors that show up in our social settings that have a bearing on how others react to us, as to whether we are accepted or rejected. I recall once seeing lists in a sociology textbook that identified some of the factors that could hinder or help one to have social success. The authors had no intention of attaching any religious significance to them, but I was struck by the fact that every one of them was rooted within the Scripture—and that the mature Christian would already be working on those very things. Almost any trait that would affect how others treat us can be found in the Bible. The Creator made us; he knows what works. Think about some of them:

Shyness and timidity. The Bible tells us that he

who would have friends must show himself to be friendly (Proverbs 18:24).

Holding grudges. Acquaintances withhold acceptance if they know they are under the microscope of those who look for reasons to justify their grudges. Remember in 1 Samuel 18:9 that "Saul eyed David from that day." All the passages on forgiveness come into play here also, such as: Matthew 6:14–15; Luke 17:3–4; Colossians 3:12–13; and Ephesians 4:31–32.

Gossiping. Gossipers are insecure and hope to elevate themselves by tearing others down, but they are rejected by friends who know they will be their next victims. Read James 3:1ff and passages that deal with tale bearing and back biting, such as: Leviticus 19:16; Proverbs 11:13, 20:19, 26:20–22, 15:1–4, 25:23; and Romans 1:30. Remember: "You don't have to take back what you don't say," and "Things left unsaid are not repeated."

Jealousy. There is a wholesome jealousy, such as God has, but the type that causes rejection and alienates is defined as being "resentfully suspicious and envious." It leads to "pain felt and malignity conceived at the sight of excellence on the part of another." Wholesome love is free of taint and jealousy, 1 Corinthians 13:4–7. The fruit of the Spirit is very sweet, Galatians 5:19–23.

Ridicule of Others. If you were to ask a class of young people to list their pet peeves, I can assure you that a number of them will say they don't like "People who think they are better than I am and who put me down." Ironically, a number of them will have in mind the others who are writing the same things! In this connection, it would help us to compose a character sketch of the Pharisee in Luke 18:9–11 and to read also the warnings about showing respect of persons in James 2:1–9.

Boastfulness and Bragging. Society in general dislikes the person who "toots his own horn," exalts himself, and flaunts wealth, status, and achievement. All the scriptures that deal with God's grace and our unworthiness should put this trait in focus for us, such as: Ephesians 2:8–10; 1 Timothy 1:12–17 and 1 Corinthians 15:10. It is easy for one to deceive himself with a high personal opinion of self, Galatians 6:3; Philippians 2:3; 1 Peter 5:5; Proverbs 3:34 and 6:17.

An Argumentative, Contentious Spirit. Even though truth must be loved and honorably defended, an offensive spirit that alienates without reason or charity causes rejection. Paul often faced unreasoning opposition to truth (2 Thessalonians 3:1–2), and John rebuked the malicious words of Diotrophes (3 John 9–11). Paul warned Timothy to avoid strife, 2 Timothy 2:23–25.

Sarcasm and Unkind Speech. Sometimes people seek to cut and hurt deliberately; with others, the hurt may be the result of a misguided attempt to be clever at the expense of another. Sarcasm alienates. Speech is to be free from bitterness, wrath, and anger (Ephesians 4:29–32). Christians are taught to control their speech (James 3; Colossians 4:6).

FACTORS THAT HELP SOCIAL ACCEPTANCE

Dependability. Normal people eventually will shun one who is careless about fulfilling assignments or duties. Offensive behavior shows up as chronic tardiness, failure to return borrowed items, or failure to respect confidences or keep promises. Paul expected others to be dependable (Philippians 2:12; 2 Thessalonians 3:4), and he was careful to see that others could maintain confidence in him (2 Corinthians 8:18–21). "God has no larger field for the man who is not faithfully doing his work where he is." Sometimes congregations are not dependable. Their irresponsibility shows up in tardiness about paying their bills, failure to communicate with the missionaries they support, carelessness about answering their mail, and thoughtlessness about support of their minister and staff members.

Cheerfulness. Gloomy, depressed crepe hangers do not attract friends. The happy, smiling Christian with a winsome personality is a magnet that others like to be around. We all know lonely souls who ache for companionship, but they drive away friends who cannot take another depressing rehearsal of ailments they have heard already a number of times. "A merry heart does good like a medicine, but a broken spirit dries the bones." (Proverbs 17:22). The medical community is giving fresh emphasis to the therapeutic value of laughter. Christians can be happy in burdensome circumstances when others cannot, James 1:2–3. Charles Buxton once said, "You haven't fulfilled every duty until you have fulfilled the duty of being pleasant."

Honest Compliments. Notice that this refers to "honest" compliments for those who deserve them. Otherwise, it is flattery, which the Bible strongly condemns.

While we are thinking about compliments, we need to guard against the two-edged compliment:

"Isn't it nice that they are finally putting some style in larger sizes."

"That dress seems to become you even more as you get older."

"It's been years since I've seen you! You've held up well, but I still wouldn't have recognized you if it hadn't been for your suit!"

Have you noticed how Paul usually began his epistles with words of commendation? (See Philippians 1:3–6; Colossians 1:3–8; 1 Thessalonians 1:2–5; 2 Thessalonians 1:3–8). If he couldn't commend them for what they had done, he commended them for what God had done for them! (1 Corinthians 1:4–8)

Fairness and Recognition of Others' Rights. We regard a person who takes digs at others or cannot take criticism as a "poor sport." A person who will not give credit to others because of narrow prejudice loses friends. We do not have to agree with others' bad philosophy in order to be fair-minded. One man described another very opinionated member as being "so narrow minded that he can look through a keyhole with both eyes at the same time!" The Golden Rule imposes on us the duty to be fair (Matthew 7:12).

Thoughtfulness and Preparedness for Duty. Some are never prepared. They are scatterbrained and lackadaisical about the future. They become free loaders and moochers who do not bear their fair share of group duties. Those who are appreciated are those who want to do their part, as the Macedonians did in 2 Corinthians

8:1-5. Paul treasured the help of the Philippians as they wanted to have a part with him in his good work, from the first day (Philippians 4:14-19).

In training our children, our best approach is to quit modeling these traits that hinder acceptance and model in a positive way those that attract friends.

THE GREATEST CONCERN: SPIRITUAL ACCEPTANCE

We should be grateful that God accepts all who desire to be with him. He is "the God of a second chance!" Jesus made that clear to the woman in John 8 who was caught in an adulterous act. He told her to "Go, and sin no more." He gave encouragement to a thief who was crucified with him (Luke 23:39-43). Peter was used to offer salvation to Cornelius. He learned that "God shows no partiality, but in every nation, he that fears him and works righteousness is accepted by him" (Acts 10:34-35).

God's teaching on grace (Ephesians 2:1-10) encourages us. Paul's experience with God's grace is a good model of how it works (1 Timothy 1:15-17). The Corinthians had once been saturated in an immoral world, but they had been cleansed and accepted by God (1 Corinthians 6:9-11). The very ones who had clamored for the crucifixion of Jesus were offered remission of sins if they would repent and put Christ on in baptism (Acts 2:36-38). So, God promises to accept us through Christ.

As a congregation of his people, we are taught to be accepting of all others who want to come to Christ also.

Showing respect of persons dishonors others and makes us sinners (James 2:1–9). We are taught to reject radicalism and extremism (2 Timothy 2:23). Healthy, mature Christians will not feel the hurt of being rejected—neither will they cause others to feel that hurt by demonstrating snobbish, self-righteousness. They will keep growing in love and joy. A wealth of practical information is found in Romans 12 and 13 to make us more lovable people that others want to be around. If we will read those chapters with serious meditation often, we will be surprised at how much easier it is to think elevated thoughts about others.

The greatest joy any of us will ever know is acceptance by God as one of his for Eternity: "... the King will say to those on his right hand, 'Come, you blessed of my Father, inherit the kingdom prepared for you from the foundation of the world'" (Matthew 25:34).

QUESTIONS FOR DISCUSSION

1. Discuss the need of small children to feel loved and accepted in a family. What can new parents-to-be do before a child is born to prepare themselves better for the arrival of a child?
2. As children grow, what are some things that could happen that cause them to question their acceptance in a family?
3. Can you identify some "childhood hurts" you observed as you grew up? In hindsight, do you

feel any were exaggerated in your mind at the time?
4. Discuss the tendency of the world to regard externals, such as money, athletic ability, intelligence, and beauty, as conditions of acceptance. To what degree may Christians legitimately desire these externals in their lives?
5. How may self-esteem be wisely nurtured in children without causing them to be adversely affected by distorted concepts?
6. What comes to your mind about any of the items that hinder or help social acceptance? Are there other things not in the lists that you feel should be added to it?
7. As you thought about the factors that help social acceptance, is there any one of the factors that you feel deserves greater attention and implementation than the others?
8. If "our greatest concern" should be spiritual readiness to be accepted by God, discuss some things which you feel deserve more attention in our lives in today's busy world.

2
THE POWER OF A BIBLICAL SELF-IMAGE
BILL BAGENTS

Many good people believe that the root of all sin is pride—thinking too much of ourselves and too little of God. Genesis 3 reports how the serpent planted doubts about God's goodness, implying that, by forbidding the fruit of the tree, God was somehow holding humans back and denying their full potential. That ancient account is the first of the Bible's stout and frequent warnings about the dangers of pride.

- "The wicked in his proud countenance does not seek God. God is in none of his thoughts" (Psalm 10:4).
- "God resists the proud, but gives grace to the humble" (Proverbs 3:34; James 4:6; 1 Peter 5:5).
- "Pride goes before destruction, and a haughty spirit before a fall" (Proverbs 16:18).
- "For I say, through the grace given to me, to

everyone who is among you, not to think of himself more highly than he ought to think …" (Romans 12:3).
- "Do not set your mind on high things, but associate with the humble. Do not be wise in your own opinion" (Romans 12:16).
- "For if anyone thinks himself to be something, when he is nothing, he deceives himself" (Galatians 6:3).

In addition to these verses, many Bible stories also oppose pride. Absalom satisfied his ego by having fifty men run before his chariot (2 Samuel 15:1). Haman's dream of self-elevation included a royal robe which the king had worn, a horse on which the king had ridden, and a parade through the city square (Esther 6:7–9). Herod's ego was stroked as citizens flattered him with "The voice of a god, and not of a man" (Acts 13:22). And each of these men came to a terrible end. Nebuchadnezzar's self-flattery did not cost him his life, but it earned stout rebuke from God (Daniel 4:28–37).

Pride invites destruction. Pride invites God's opposition. Pride ensures an extra measure of life's hurts. Knowing that, both faith and good sense tell us to reject pride and choose humility. To avoid certain and unnecessary pain, don't seek to elevate self (Proverbs 25:27, 27:2; Luke 14:7–11, 20:45–47). Scripture could not be clearer: "He who exalts himself will be humbled, and he who humbles himself will be exalted" (Luke 14:11). There's great wisdom in listening to God and preventing self-caused hurt.

ON THE OTHER HAND

As Christians, we're acutely aware of our failings and weaknesses. We know the scathing truth of Romans 3:9-18. We especially know Romans 3:23, "... For all have sinned and fall short of the glory of God."

Not only do we struggle with sin issues and pride problems, we also don't do well at directing our own lives. Jeremiah 10:23 still tells us, "O Lord, I know the way of man is not in himself; it is not in man who walks to direct his own steps." Proverbs 14:12 still reads, "There is a way that seems right to a man, but its end is the way of death." And "Every way of a man is right in his own eyes, but the Lord weighs the hearts" (Proverbs 21:2). Our sins put Jesus on the cross (Romans 5:6-11). We were hopelessly dead. We were enemies of God (Ephesians 2:1-10). Just look at humanity's track record throughout Scripture or history. Just look at today's news!

A wise man once said, "The devil doesn't care whether he gets us coming or going." That is a fiercely accurate statement. Satan is happy to use pride to destroy. He will give us today if we'll give him our future. But, he's just as happy to overcome us at the other extreme. People who count themselves worthless will not be zealous soldiers of the cross.

There's not an ounce of sympathy in Satan. He loves to discourage. He loves to destroy. He loves to tempt people to judge themselves by impossible standards. He loves to catch people in the trap of letting others control their feelings. He doesn't care which message it takes. All of us have heard his lies:

- You're not good enough.
- Nobody loves you.
- You don't fit it.
- You have no talent.
- You have no purpose.
- You have nothing to contribute.
- You're too old or too young or too simple or too plain.
- If people knew the real you, they'd laugh.

I believe the devil knows how much these lies can hurt. But, he's the master of pain. I believe he takes the most delight in the pain he causes good people to inflict on themselves.

A CALL TO BIBLICAL BALANCE

We love the beautiful balance of scripture. While Romans 12:3 rightly warns us not to think too highly of ourselves, other passages remind us that there is a healthy, God given sense of self-image. There's a measured, limited, and healthy sense of caring for ourselves so that we can serve God and bless others.

- Faced with the most important mission ever conceived, Jesus invited His apostles to practice essential self-care: "Come aside by

yourselves to a deserted place and rest a while" (Mark 6:31).
- The second command states, "You shall love your neighbor as yourself" (Leviticus 19:18, Matthew 22:39).
- "So, husbands ought to love their own wives as their own bodies: he who loves his wife loves himself. For no one ever hates his own flesh, but nourishes and cherishes it, even as the Lord does the church" (Ephesians 5:28–29). Again, this must be held in balance with the warning of 2 Timothy 3:1–5.
- "Let nothing be done through selfish ambition or conceit, but in lowliness of mind let each esteem others better than himself. Let each of you look out not only for his own interests, but also for the interests of others" (Philippians 2:3–4).

Galatians 6:4 speaks powerfully to this point: "But let each one examine his own work, and then he will have rejoicing in himself alone, and not in another." The concept is not "Look at me. I'm great! God is lucky to have me." Rather, the idea is "By God's grace and power, I have been blessed to serve Him" (Philippians 2:12–13; Acts 17:28).

Even the Golden Rule quietly reminds us that self-awareness can help us obey God by treating others well. "Therefore, whatever you want men to do to you, do also to them, for this is the Law and the Prophets" (Matthew 7:12). It's not wrong to have godly desire, to want to be treated well, and to use our knowledge of our own desires to show love and respect to others.

Many additional passages encourage us to remember how much God loves us. Neither arrogance nor continual self-loathing are encouraged in scripture. There's pain and harm in imbalance, extremism, and in swinging from one extreme to the other. As dangerous as pride is, forgetting how richly God has blessed us has its own unique set of dangers. We who are "fearfully and wonderfully made" have tremendous reason for gratitude before God (Psalm 139:14). We who have been "made a little lower than the angels" have tremendous resources with which to serve God (Psalm 8:5). We whom God has crowned "with glory and honor" should hardly live in misery and fear (Psalm 8:5). We whom "God so loved" and for whom "God demonstrates His love" have every reason for joy and hope (John 3:16, Romans 5:8).

What does it cost us to forget that we are made in the image of God (Genesis 1:26)?

- It will cost us our sense of purpose. We won't be able to live as the salt of the earth and the light of the world (Matthew 5:13–16). We won't remember that we are a needed and important part of the body (1 Corinthians 12:12–31; Ephesians 4:11–16).
- It will cost us gratitude. We won't have the heart to "Continue earnestly in prayer, being vigilant in it with thanksgiving" (Colossians 4:2).

- It will cost us joy. We won't be living the abundant, victorious life which Jesus came to give (John 10:10, 1 Corinthians 15:57–58).
- It will cost us the peace that surpasses understanding (John 14:27, Galatians 5:22, Philippians 4:6–7).
- In truth, forgetting that we are made in the image of God will cost us our humanity. It will cost us our souls. It will leave us believing that we are nothing more than higher-order animals.

If we forget that we have been made in the image of God, we may not even be able to accept a simple compliment. You know what the devil loves to do with sincere, legitimate compliments. He tempts us to think, "I shouldn't enjoy that. If I did, I would be prideful. I'd better reject it—FAST." We must not fall victim to such false humility! It robs us of encouragement. It robs the person who is extending the compliment of the opportunity to positively impact others (Hebrews 10:24).

It was near Christmas one year when a good brother in Christ asked my wife, Laura, "Can I give Bill a present?" After she said yes, he explained. He had once offered another preacher a gift. But the preacher didn't accept it. Evidently, he thought that it might be a hardship for a brother on a fixed income to give such a gift. I believe that he forgot Acts 20:25. Compliments, like gifts, often bless the giver even more than they bless the recipient. This world is sin damaged. It is so often hard, harsh, and negative. It beats people down. We need to hear good words from the good people in our lives. We need to accept and appreciate such words. Honest compliments aren't evil. Scripture is filled with them. Genesis 6:8 compliments Noah. In Genesis 18:16–19, the Lord highly compliments Abraham. By inspiration, Luke compliments the Bereans in Acts 17:11. Note how Paul frequently praises the faithfulness of others (Romans 1:8, 16:1–12; 1 Corinthians 16:15–18; Ephesians 6:21; Philippians 3:19–30; Colossians 1:3–8, 3:7–15; 1 Thessalonians 1:2–10)?

We're blessed to remember that Jesus was a master of encouragement through timely, sincere, and specific compliments. He said of the compassionate centurion, "Assuredly, I say to you, I have not found such great faith, no not in Israel" (Matthew 8:19). He said of a woman whom He healed, "Be of good cheer, daughter, your faith has made you well" (Matthew 9:21). He said of John the Baptizer, "Assuredly I say to you, among those born of women there has not risen one greater than John the Baptist ..." (Matthew 1:11). He complimented His faithful followers: "Here are My mother and My brothers! For whoever does the will of My Father in heaven is My brother and sister and mother" (Matthew 12:49–50). He said of the humble Canaanite woman, "O woman, great is your faith" (Matthew 15:28)! Both Jesus and Paul embodied the Encouragement Principle: "Catch people doing good and say so!" As we practice this principle, we do much to prevent the hurts of feeling unneeded, unwanted, and unloved.

FALSE PATHS TO SELF-ESTEEM

When people forget that God is the true source of our worth, they often seek validation through other means. They forget that the only "in group" that matters is the group that is saved in Christ. They forget that human approval is fickle and fleeting. The public welcomed Jesus to Jerusalem with tremendous fanfare (Luke 19:28–40). Yet, the mob called for His death shortly thereafter (Luke 22:13–25).

When people forget that God is the true source all worth, they forget what it means to "be somebody." Was the deceitful Amalekite of 1 Samuel 1 seeking funds or was he trying to make a name for himself? The rich young ruler reminds us that there's more to life than status and money (Luke 18:18–23). So does the rich man who ignored the needs of Lazarus (Luke 16:19–31). In a strange sense, Judas Iscariot became "somebody." He "earned" his fifteen minutes of fame. For a few hours, he was important to the leaders of his nation. Yet, Judas couldn't live with what he had become (Matthew 27:1–10, Acts 1:15–20). Diotrophes, the censor/controller, tried to be somebody by rejecting faithful brethren, even those who came with apostolic approval (3 John 9–10).

WHAT'S THE TRUTH?

At this point I know that you might well be wanting to ask, "So you're saying that all I have to do is to live for God and I'll be loved, valued, and accepted by everyone?" We could never say that. The sinless Son of God was Himself "despised and rejected by men" (Isaiah 53:3). He was crucified by His enemies. But we know that's not the whole story. The Lord Jesus was praised and honored by His Father (Mark 1:9–11). He was resurrected and exalted by God. One day, every knee will bow before Him and every tongue will confess that He is Lord (Philippians 2:5–11).

We stand with Him when we embrace our identity as strangers and pilgrims on this earth (Hebrews 11:13–16, 1 Peter 2:11–12). If being accepted by God means being rejected by men, we welcome their rejection (Acts 5:41, 1 Peter 4:12–19). There will come a day when God Himself will right every wrong and wipe away every tear from the eyes of those who love Him (Revelation 21:4).

QUESTIONS FOR DISCUSSION

1. Do you think more Christians are hurt by thinking too highly of themselves or too lowly of themselves? Explain your answer.
2. In what ways can it bless us to be "acutely aware of our failings" (2 Corinthians 7:8–12, Galatians 6:1–5)?
3. What kinds of impossible standards do Christians sometimes set for themselves?
4. How can the setting of impossible standards hurt us?
5. Given all our weaknesses and faults, why should Christians be strong and confident people?

6. In what ways is the ability to accept compliments a virtue? How can accepting compliments in a spirit of humility help both the giver and the recipient?
7. What advice would you give to a Christian friend who needs to develop a more biblical self-image? How could a person wisely pursue this goal?

3
THE CRITIC'S STING AND THE GOSSIP'S GORE
JACK P. WILHELM

We often hear, "Sticks and stones may break my bones but words can never hurt me." Someone has said that whoever said that was probably hard of hearing. We all admit there is perhaps a bit of truth in that saying, but we also all know that it's not true all the time. Sometimes the vicious sting of criticism can inflict inward emotional pain on us that hurts more than a physical attack would.

People have apparently been aware of caustic hurts caused by our words in different ages. John Heywood, who lived about 1497 to 1580, said in his *Proverbs*, "It hurteth not the toung to give faire words." About a century later, George Chapman (1559?–1634) said in *Eastward Ho*, "Fair words never hurt the tongue." In recent bulletin board quotes, I have seen a later adaptation: "Sharp words cut the tongue" or "Kind words do not cut the tongue." It is a conclusion people conclude by experience even if they had not seen those earlier quotes.

Those who are victims of severe criticism probably fall into two broad categories: (1) Those who attempt to do anything, and (2) those who never attempt to do anything.

Margie Overton gave me the following short poem from an unknown author that her mother taught her in childhood:

> *Be not dismayed, nor be surprised*
> *If what you do is criticized.*
> *Mistakes are made, we can't deny—*
> *But only made by folks who try.*

One time a man was criticized for failing to provide for his family. Times were hard. He could not find a job, although some questioned how seriously he was looking. He decided to go into the fish business. He liked to fish and thought he could mix business with pleasure.

After his first catch, he set up shop underneath a sign he made: "Fresh Fish for Sale Today!" The first passerby offered a criticism: "Why would you use the word Today? Everyone knows you don't want to sell them yesterday or tomorrow. That leaves only today to sell them."

So, he sawed off that last word and mounted the new version: "Fresh Fish for Sale." The next passerby asked, "Why use the word Fresh? Do you mean to imply that at other times the fish are not fresh?" Again, he changed his sign. Now it said, "Fish for Sale."

The next critic said, "Why not leave off the words For Sale? Any numbskull would know that's why you have a fish market?" Finally, he wound up with only the word "Fish." Even then, he still had a critic! The next passerby said, "Why do you need to put up a sign at all? Anyone who comes within half a mile of this place knows from the smell what you are selling!" We are reminded that the folks who are determined to "leave no turn unstoned" will find something to criticize about any endeavor one undertakes.

Unreasonable critics, who may be using the only talent they have, might be wise to think about an observation made by Jean Sibelius: "Pay no attention to what critics say. No statue has ever been set up in honor of a critic!"

GOSSIP AND CRITICISM OFTEN GO TOGETHER

Gossipers can hurt their victims as keenly as critics. A gossiper is given to idle talk or rumor about others, especially their private affairs. What they say may or may not be true, but it can still hurt. The terms tattle and talebearer are closely related. Tattlers and talebearers often tell things private or secret about others out of spite. They are strongly condemned in the Bible in such verses as these:

- You shall not go about as a talebearer among your people ... (Leviticus 19:16).
- A talebearer reveals secrets, but he who is of a faithful spirit conceals a matter (Proverbs 11:13).

- The words of a talebearer are like tasty trifles, and they go down into the inmost body. (Proverbs 18:8). [Literally rooms of the belly. We would say they hurt you "down deep."] A similar proverb is in 26:22.
- He who goes about as a talebearer reveals secrets; therefore, do not associate with one who flatters with his lips (Proverbs 20:19).
- Where there is no talebearer, the strife ceases (Proverbs 26:20). [Congregations sometimes suffer irreparable harm because of talebearers. Elders have been warned to try to control them, Titus 1:10–16.]
- Paul rebuked some in the early church who "learn to be idle, wandering about from house to house, and not only idle but also gossips and busybodies, saying things they ought not" (1 Timothy 5:13). [There was a time when a gossip was one's closest friend, a confidant to whom one could discuss his or her most private thoughts, as illustrated by Lady McBeth who had a "gossip" to unburden her heart to. In the passing of time, the gossips became blabbermouths who passed on morsels of confidential information to the hurt of their former friends.]

If anything, an unbridled gossiper is more unethical and potentially more dangerous than the bold critic. A critic may differ with us openly, face to face; the gossip may spread his or her venom behind our backs. The gossip can wound us without our knowing it. Their stunned listeners are bewildered, not knowing what to believe, but always view the victims with raised eyebrows of suspicion.

CLARIFYING SOME FALSE ASSUMPTIONS

Sometimes overly sensitive souls infer some uncomfortable conclusions when they feel the critic's sting or the gore of the gossip for the first time.

We should not assume that all who are criticized are actually guilty. Human nature sometimes makes us leap at thinking the worst about one, especially if a victim does not rebound with a fiery denial and a quick defense. We say, "Where there's smoke, there's bound to be fire!" What we learn about love from 1 Corinthians 13 should tell us not to be so hasty to "believe all things." After all, think of all the honorable Bible characters who were criticized unjustly—like Joseph and Paul and even Jesus himself.

We should not assume that one might as well go ahead and indulge in questionable behavior as to be blamed for it anyway. Joseph could have rationalized this way when falsely accused by Potiphar's wife, but he said, "How can I do this great wickedness, and sin against God?" (Genesis 39:9)

We should not assume the worst about ourselves because we are criticized. Many say, "I cannot understand why this has happened to me. I try to live right and be a good person. Maybe I'm not really doing right; otherwise, why would God allow something like this to happen to me?" Job's friends socked him heavily with a charge of wrongdoing. It was as if they were saying, "Job, we know that wrongdoers suffer. You're suffering, so you must be a wrongdoer and trying to hide it from us." We know that there was another explanation for it and that, by not giving up, Job eventually was vindicated. (Read Job 42:9-10 and James 5:11). The need that everyone has to repent is not equated with his personal guilt, as Jesus explained in Luke 13:3-5.

We should not assume that unjust criticism gives us a special license to do as we please. The temptation is strong to say, "What I do is strictly my personal business. I do not care what others say or think." Christians are taught, however, to abstain from doing things that will harm their influence and harm the church. Read 1 Corinthians 10:32; Galatians 5:13-17; Matthew 5:13-16; 1 Corinthians 8:9-13; and Romans 14:15-21. These verses plainly teach that there is a duty to show "brotherly love" in situations where we could actually do harm by engaging in questionable activity.

A word of caution is needed here though! We know that there are some cantankerous souls who have learned that there are certain things they can do without and take it upon themselves to dictate optional preferences as if they were God's law. They claim to be a "weak brother" who is offended when you do something they have learned to do without. It may not be wrong in itself. It's just not their thing! Does that mean that we must always defer to every crank? Not really. The main question, of course, is whether the action is right or wrong in itself. If it is not inherently and scripturally wrong, then this principle does not require us to forego enjoyment of a scriptural, permissible activity to pacify some stubborn critic. If a person knows enough to object to some activity that he says offends him, he is not in the category of a weak brother!

We should not assume that objective, honest criticism never has any benefit. If we bristle at all criticism and become defensive, we may miss out on some valuable help, while running the risk of being hardened in wrongdoing. There are some types of criticism that can help us.

We can benefit by rebukes for sin that are offered with a good attitude by people who really care about us, Galatians 6:1; 2:11. The critic is not always our adversary. It may be the person who cares most about us!

Children are wise to heed the counsel of loving parents, Ephesians 6:1–4. At times, I have had teenagers complain about some restriction imposed by their parents. We may have a conversation like the following:

I say, "How old are you?"
They may say, "I'm 15."
"How old is your dad?"
"Oh, he's an old man, 40 at least!"
"Which of you two then has had the most experience in life and should be best qualified to teach the other? You don't know what it's like to be 40, but he knows what it's like to be 15, plus he has learned a lot in all those years between 15 and 40. You better listen to him. He's got the edge on you there!"

Usually, thinking young people will agree. If they still seem a bit cynical, I may then add another counseling gem that I have found that works well: I say, "Name one thing for me that your parents (teachers) have ever asked you to do but that it would help you be a better Christian boy (or girl)?" If we're dealing with Christians who say our greatest aim is to please the Lord and be Christlike, their own honest answer to this question usually puts it in focus for them.

Further, we are also benefited by corrections that are shown to us by concerned friends and teachers. In Acts 18:24–28, Apollos was a great preacher apparently, but he was deficient in knowledge about a critical issue that Aquila and Priscilla "explained to him more perfectly." Whatever Aquila and Priscilla had to say, it was an information exchange that worked to the advantage of Apollos. By listening, his future service was much more effective than it would have been had he bristled with stubborn rejection of their counsel.

In a broader sense, sometimes doctrinal errors have to be pointed out to the uninformed by more mature, experienced gospel ministers who are charged with the responsibility of rebuke. Saul of Tarsus had to accept truth and change before he could ever be the peerless Apostle Paul! He later rebuked Peter (Galatians 2:11), and always pointed idol worshippers to the true God (1 Thessalonians 1:9, 2:13). Most ministers can tell you of honest souls who have been forever grateful to the soul winners or evangelists who shared the true gospel with them to help them abandon former error.

THE CRITIC'S STING AND THE GOSSIP'S GORE

SUGGESTIONS FOR COPING SUCCESSFULLY WITH CRITICISM

- Sometimes it helps us to take the initiative. Ask in advance for a critique and suggestions for improvement. This diffuses the critic and turns him/her into an ally by putting the ball in his court. Of course, we should be sincere when we make this offer to listen.
- Be realistic. Some criticism is going to be unavoidable. It might help to remember that even Jesus, the Son of God, was a victim! He learned from his indignities (Hebrews 5:8–9), but they still came:

He was criticized because of his family background: "Is not this the carpenter's son?" (Matthew 13:54–57)

He was criticized because of the community from which he came: "Can any good thing come out of Nazareth?" (John 1:46). On one occasion, an outspoken church lady nixed a preacher who was being interviewed by a congregation by saying, "I know the community he's from and some of the people he grew up with and can't believe he could help us."

He was criticized for his association with sinners: "Why does your master eat with publicans and sinners?" (Matthew 9:11; Luke 7:36–50, and 5:31–32).

He was criticized even for doing good things in a way that differed from the expectations of others: He healed on the Sabbath in a setting where he violated traditions of men but not laws of God (Mark 2:23–28).

- We need to realize that those who would be like Jesus will also be the victims as he was. Jesus told his disciples that offenses would be unavoidable (Luke 17:1) and that those who were ignorant would mistreat those who did know him (John 16:1–3). When Paul encouraged Timothy to "endure hardness as a good soldier of Jesus Christ," he used the examples of the soldier, the athlete, and the hard working farmer to show how it helps to have an understanding in advance that some things just don't go right, even for the best Christian on earth! (2 Timothy 2:3–7) Disciples are not immune to the sting of the critic and the gore of the gossip, as Jesus said in Matthew 5:10–12: He warned that they will "say all kinds of evil against you falsely."
- We need to realize that criticism is endurable and that it is possible to cope with it victoriously. We are promised that God will "make a way of escape" for those who are steadfastly faithful (1 Corinthians 10:13). Peter declared firmly that Christians do not have to render "evil for evil or reviling for reviling" (1 Peter 3:9). Human nature prods us to "give them as good as they send!" But how can we find the strength to act like we know we should?

OTHER SUGGESTIONS FOR COPING

Know its source. The false, vicious charge is "earthly, sensual, devilish" (James 3:14–18). Attacks of that nature are from mentally ill misfits who do not know the difference between maturity and sniveling littleness. Or it may be that the onslaught comes from one so wicked that he/she is not capable of sound reasoning. Paul had to deal with some like that (2 Thessalonians 3:1–3). Occasionally one may still have enough conscience to "be ashamed" (1 Peter 3:16) when the victim reacts with calm control, but at least, knowing the source can often help you make allowances for it and remain silent.

Know its cause. It may be because you have taken a stand for Christ that opposition comes, or as he said, "for my sake" (Matthew 5:11). Or it may be rooted in some effort to keep Christians from telling others about Christ, as the first disciples were threatened (Acts 5:23–30). Or it may be rooted in jealousy and envy because of your success, as Paul and Barnabas experienced in Acts 13:44–45. It will become apparent to you, the longer you live, that some can weep with you a lot easier than they can rejoice with you. The higher you set your standards, the more you may become a target for the envious.

Know your own heart and motives. Jesus set his goal to "always do those things that please him" (John 8:29). If you keep your motive honorable and your conscience clear, and at least try to do something constructive, the attacks of the critic will not be able to sidetrack you. For a long time, many people have been encouraged by the philosophy of Abraham Lincoln:

If I were to read, much less answer, all attacks made on me, this shop might as well be closed for any other business. I do the very best I know how, the very best I can, and I mean to keep doing so until the end. If the end brings me out all right, what is said against me won't amount to anything. If the end brings me out wrong, then 10 angels swearing I was right would make no difference.

WHEN IS ENOUGH ENOUGH?

Generally, "a loud attempt to excuse helps those who accuse." But there may be a time when we still have to "clear the air." If truth is slandered, giving a wisely worded constructive rebuttal may be unavoidable. Paul found himself in that situation at times. In Romans 3:1–8, Paul referred to a matter in which he had been "slanderously reported" as saying, "Let us do evil that good may come." He felt constrained to deny it. Almost all of 2 Corinthians involved a defense against vicious accusations that Paul would have preferred not to have to deal with. (See 1 Corinthians 4:17–21, 9:1–23; and 2 Corinthians 3:1–2, 8:20-23, 10:8–18, and 11:5–31). Peter urged Christians to "be ready to give a defense" regarding those who "speak evil of you as evildoers," so that "those who revile your good conduct in Christ may be ashamed" (1 Peter 3:15–16).

By nature, Christians are generally peaceable people who do not like controversy. We are taught that when unfair criticism comes, our best defense is to "endure grief, suffering wrongfully," and that it is "commendable before God to take it patiently" (1 Peter 2:19-20). If Christians can show by a good life that they are following the example of Christ, they will have respect—and at least great inner peace that they are like Jesus.

"When he was reviled, he did not revile in return; when he suffered, he did not threaten, but committed himself to him who judges righteously" (1 Peter 2:23-24).

QUESTIONS FOR DISCUSSION

1. What is your evaluation of the expression, "Sticks and stones may hurt my bones, but words can never hurt me"? Are there times and ways that words can cause a hurt deeper than physical wounds?
2. Is there a difference in "gossiping" and in legitimately sharing news items or facts about others? What guidelines might be followed to know when to discuss such matters?
3. Have you ever been helped personally by a criticism? A job evaluation that you took to heart? A friend's direct suggestion about something you needed to know?
4. Share any tactful approach that you have found helpful in offering or receiving constructive criticism.
5. Are there some professionals that receive a higher level of criticism, such as coaches, preachers, teachers, administrators, and politicians? Discuss how criticism is often

meted out to these and the fairness or unfairness of its effects on them and their spouses and children.
6. Is a person ever justified in saying, "I don't care what anybody says. My life is my own and I will live it as I please, regardless of what happens"?
7. By thinking about the first Christians, what specific Bible examples or verses have you found to be helpful in coping with criticism?
8. What situations might exist that you feel justify a Christian or the church in answering false charges publicly to "clear the air and set the record straight"?

4

WHEN GOOD WORDS DON'T COME

BILL BAGENTS

We all need to hear encouraging words. Mark Twain is credited with saying, "I could live a month on a good compliment." Obviously, Twain exaggerated for effect. He wanted to stress the power of good words. I believe he gave us credit for knowing that people need encouraging far more often than once a month.

Scripture clearly shows that God recognizes our need for encouraging words. The Lord spoke such words to Joshua as he began his tenure as Israel's leader following the death of Moses (Joshua 1:1–9). God's angel called Gideon to judgeship through encouraging words (Judges 6:11–16). John 14 records some of the many wonderfully encouraging words spoken by Jesus. Virtually all of Paul's letters begin with strong encouragement (See Romans 1:8; 1 Corinthians 1:4–9).

What happens if the encouraging words which we

need to hear do not come? What if they don't come when we need them? What if they don't come at all? When they don't, we have encountered another of life's hurts. Wisdom demands that we work to minimize that hurt.

INEFFECTIVE ATTEMPTS TO MINIMIZE THE HURT

One ineffective attempt to mask our pain over the absence of encouraging words is to pretend that we don't need them. I love good fiction. It can be both healthy and entertaining—for a brief time—to get lost in the world of the imagination. I don't love self-deception. There's nothing good to say for it. Nothing good comes from a lie.

Truth is precious. It's so precious that Jesus could describe Himself as "the way, the truth, and the life" (John 14:6). Proverbs 23:23 urges the faithful, "Buy the truth, and do not sell it, also wisdom and instruction and understanding." In Ephesians 4:25, Paul urges each Christian "to speak truth with his neighbor." Surely, we owe ourselves the same consideration.

Telling ourselves that we don't need encouraging words may either stem from or help to create a "martyr complex." It can tempt us to take on a victim mentality. Neither is part of healthy Christian living.

Such self-deception is, at best, a temporary fix. It's fraught with danger. It's an illusion which cannot last. Even if it did, it would not bless us.

A second ineffective approach to hiding our hurt over the absence of encouraging words is "to blow our own horns." Maybe you have heard it said like this: "If you don't talk good about yourself, then nobody will." I doubt that. At the same time, I think you will agree that virtually no one likes a braggart.

Proverbs 27:2 wisely advises, "Let another man praise you and not your own mouth; a stranger, and not your own lips." No explanation follows in the text of Proverbs 27. Perhaps that is because none is needed. I believe Solomon gives us credit for knowing just how bad self-congratulation sounds. It sounds almost as bad as the closely related practice of "fishing for compliments." I appreciate wisdom of the fellow who said, "If you have to fish for your compliments, then they ain't worth catchin'."

A third ineffective attempt to hide our hurt over the absence of good words is to tell ourselves, "I'll show them. I'll do so much good that they will have to notice. They'll have to say something then!"

As much as we might wish this were true, it is not. Paul's critics never praised him for preaching without pay in Corinth. In fact, they used his sacrifice to question his apostleship (1 Corinthians 9; 2 Corinthians 12:11–21). The Pharisees didn't commend Jesus for His miracles, not even for the raising of the dead!

This line of bad thinking has other difficulties, too. It leads us dangerously close to the terrible "mistake of motive" which Jesus warned against in His Sermon on the Mount (Matthew 6:1–5 and 16–18). At least three times, the Lord tells us that those who seek the praise of men have all the reward that they will ever get. Those who seek the glory of the Father will be rewarded by Him.

A fourth ineffective response to disappointment over the absence of encouraging words often begins with the following self-talk: "I did well, and nobody noticed I did well, and nobody said a thing. I won't be hurt again. I'll show them; I'll quit!"

Quitting is not an option for believers. We have the promise of Galatians 6:9: "In due season we shall reap if we do not lose heart." We have the promise of Colossians 3:23-24. We know that if we serve the Lord Christ, we shall receive the greatest of rewards from him. What could be better than hearing the Master say, "Well done, good and faithful servant" (Matthew 25:21 and 23)? Doing good to the glory of God is part of our very identity in Christ. "For we are his workmanship, created in Christ Jesus for good works, which God prepared beforehand that we should walk in them" (Ephesians 2:10). The Father sent His only begotten Son, "who gave Himself for us, that He might redeem us from every lawless deed and purify for Himself His own special people, zealous for good works" (Titus 2:14). We dare not deny who we are in Christ!

EASING THE HURT GOD'S WAY

The first key has already been noticed in Galatians 6:9 and Colossians 3:23-24. We can remember God's faithful promises. When we hurt because those around us don't seem to notice our effort for good, we can confidently remind ourselves that God never misses any good work. The Lord Jesus is in heaven right now preparing a place for those who love Him (John 14:1–4).

The day of judgment will be a day of great reward for those who stand faithful in Christ. Through the endless joy of heaven, we will never regret any good thing which we were blessed to do for our Master. Whenever we do good to the glory of God, every encouragement of Scripture is ours!

Sadly, some Christians find themselves unable to hear the encouraging words which God offers in Scripture. Some Christians have great difficulty hearing words of encouragement from any source. Why? You might want to refer to Chapter 2 in this book. The negative power of an unbiblical self-image can be devastating. False humility, fear of flattery, and pride can leave a Christian unable to hear the encouragement offered by others. A second key is found in Luke 17:5–10. We can clarify and align our own motives. Verse 10 reads, "So likewise, when you have done all those things which you are commanded say, 'We are unprofitable servants. We have done what was our duty to do.'" We don't serve God for the praise of men.

We do rejoice when men see our good works and glorify our Father in heaven (Matthew 5:16). But we know that God owes us no praise. If we did all that we could for as long as we lived, we would never be able to begin repaying God for the gift of His Son. We count it a wondrous privilege to serve the One who is saving us.

A third key is found in 1 Samuel 30:6. We can choose to encourage ourselves. Disappointment and fatigue were weighing heavily on David. While he and his men were away in battle, raiders took their families and stole all their possessions. The loss was so great that David's own men wanted to stone him. In this dark hour, "David strengthened himself in the Lord his God."

How did David strengthen (encourage) himself in the Lord? The text does not say. Surely, he prayed. As we read the Psalms, we know that he must have poured out his heart and his hurt to God in prayer. Likely, he remembered God's good favor from the past. The Lord who delivered him from the "paw of the lion and from the paw of the bear" and from the hand of the giant could deliver him again (1 Samuel 17:37).

As the sweet psalmist of Israel, it is likely that David even sang of God's goodness and mercy. Weren't Paul and Silas encouraging themselves in the Lord as they worshipped in song in the Philippian jail (Acts 16:25)? When no one else had a good word for him, David looked to the Lord. He found encouragement in God's faithful love.

A fourth key is illustrated by 1 Samuel 23:16. We can work to prevent the absence of encouragement. The Bible says, "And Jonathan, Saul's son, arose and went to David in the woods, and strengthened his hand in God." Jonathan could not have done this lightly. Saul had already asked his son and his servants to kill David (1 Samuel 19:1). Jonathan knew the risk of opposing his father's evil will (1 Samuel 20:30–34). Why, then, did Jonathan encourage his friend?

We are confident that one reason Jonathan came to his friend was that Jonathan himself was a man of faith and honor. His action was in keeping with his character. We are just as confident that Jonathan encouraged David because of the friendship they shared. They had forged a relationship which could stand up to the greatest of pressure.

Friendships like that don't just happen. Proverbs 18:24 reads, "A man who has friends must himself be friendly. But there is a friend who sticks closer than a brother." When it comes to friends, people of similar values are attracted to each other. Mutual love for the Lord drew David and Jonathan together.

We all know that we need a Jonathan in our lives. We need at least one friend who will reach out to us even in the darkest of times. There is no better place to find such friends than within the body of Christ. Within that great body, we are wise to cultivate deep relationships. That is one wise, proactive step which we can take to prevent the hurt caused by a lack of encouragement.

A fifth key is suggested by Galatians 6:7. We can invite encouragement by being encouragers. Paul wrote, "Do not be deceived, God is not mocked; for whatever a man sows, that he will also reap." The next verse makes the ultimate application. "For he who sows to his flesh, will of the flesh reap corruption, but he who sows to the Spirit will of the Spirit reap everlasting life." We also know that the law of sowing and reaping has strong application for daily life.

It is sometimes called "The Law of Reciprocity." We've all seen it in operation. Even the people of this world tend to treat us like we treat them. If we're polite, they're polite. If we're encouraging, they're encouraging.

It's a law that we can put to work in our lives. By raising our own individual "encouragement quotients," we can invite others to be encouraging toward us.

We know that "The Law of Reciprocity" is sometimes reduced to what some have called the Silver Rule: Treat others like they treat you. In light of Matthew 7:12, we reject the inferior standard of a Silver Rule. At the same time, we happily embrace God's law of sowing and reaping. By doing good, we are often able to bring out the best in others.

Knowing the power and value of encouraging others, why don't we do a better job of it? Perhaps we have never cultivated the habit of encouragement. We see the opportunity. We feel the impulse. But, somehow, we just don't put our good feelings into action. The Bible clearly tells us that thought without action won't get the job done (James 2:14-26). Perhaps shyness, fear of embarrassment, or procrastination causes some to withhold encouragement. Whatever the reason, the effect is the same. We fail to do the good that we could do, and we let down those who need us.

FINAL WORDS

As much as we need and appreciate the encouragement of others, we are wise to remember that the favor of God always matters more. John 12:42–43 is one of the saddest sentences in all of Scripture. "Nevertheless, even among the rulers many believed in Him, but because of the Pharisees they did not confess Him, lest they should be put out of the synagogue; for they loved the praise of men more than the praise of God." They sacrificed the best for a pale imitation. They sacrificed the eternal for the immediate and fleeting.

The praise of men is nothing when compared to the favor of God. Men's praise can be mere flattery (Acts 12:20-24). Sometimes it can be earned by "the tickling of itching ears" (1 Timothy 4:1-5, Luke 6:26). We dare not let any hurt cause us to forget Who is first!

While we must always value the praise of God more than the praise of men, we dare not fail to appreciate those who encourage us. Encouraging words should be acknowledged. Failing to do so may well hurt the good people who have taken the time to help us. It surely won't encourage them to keep up their efforts!

It's such a blessing to express our gratitude to those who lift us up. Expressing our thanks works to perpetuate the cycle of joy. It's one more way we remind ourselves of the power of doing good.

QUESTIONS FOR DISCUSSION

1. Is it true that we all need to hear encouraging words? Give reasons for your answer.
2. What are the key dangers of trying to meet our need for "good words" by bragging on ourselves?
3. Is it possible for us to "do so much good" that others will have to notice and say so? Explain.
4. How might we strengthen ourselves in the Lord like David did?

5. In your judgment, why are we not more consistent in encouraging our brethren? Our families?
6. What steps could we take to raise our own individual "encouragement quotients"?

THE LOVE TRAPS
JACK P. WILHELM

How do you define love? Is it the exciting tingles that cause us to feel indescribable warm fuzzies? Is it the cerebral agitation that makes us turn emotional somersaults? Or as a dictionary says, is it "strong affection for another rising out of kinship or personal ties?" Usually "warm attachment, enthusiasm, or devotion involving unselfish loyal, benevolent concern for the good of others" is included also as part of the definition.

Regardless of how we define it, almost everyone regards love as a plus in life. It is almost synonymous with pleasure in the thinking of most people. Sometimes the psychiatrists seem to imply that it is an essential to good health and survival. If so, then why is love included as a subject in a book that deals with hurts? The simple answer is that love is connected with some of the deepest hurt experienced in life as well as with some of the greatest pleasure.

Humans have been programmed with certain appetites. Those appetites have to be fed for us to be healthy. Some of our appetites are physical—and most of us give little indication that they have not been gratified excessively. Why else would we be pre-occupied with how to lose weight?

We have also spiritual appetites. Humans yearn for an inner peace "with our maker." Not all have found the truth that makes that peace possible, but we see them struggle to satisfy the appetite. There is also the emotional or psychological appetite each has to "be somebody, to be loved and appreciated." This is where love begins to play a critical role, even in the life of small babies. They cannot tell us in words yet that they yearn to be validated as a part of their families. They react though to hugs, kisses, cuddling, and joyful occasions. They seem to know whether their mothers resent them and regard them as an irritating interruption to their careers and social lives. They also know whether they are adorable and lovingly cherished, even when diapers have to be changed and spilled milk has to be mopped up.

In his book, *The Secret of Staying in Love* (Argus Communications, Niles, IL, 1974), John Powell shines a spotlight on things that often happen in the development of children that cause them to infer as they grow older that worth, love, and acceptance are conditional. If parents, especially the mother, are unwilling to express affection, are cold and go through matter-of-fact routines, are irritated by interruptions, impatient with toilet training, and communicate resentment for being tied down, babies sense that something must be wrong with them.

When all the children hear is, "If you will be quiet, if you will be good, if you will eat your dinner, not make a mess, not fuss with your brother or sister, do your chores, help around the house, stay clean, get good grades, score more points, stay out of trouble ...," they conclude that there is a price for admission to love in the family. They decide the hoop is too high for them to jump through it successfully.

Subconsciously, children often conclude that they can never meet those incessant demands, so they must be failures, unworthy even of self-love, as well as love from others. This is one of the love traps where pain shows up. A cross pull comes in which children feel that soon they will slip up and whatever love they have had tenuously extended to them will disappear. Now you are ahead of me. You are beginning to see where some hurt is coming from even in the love connection.

THE STRATEGIES OF THE LOVE STARVED

Powell continued to say that children artfully devise strategies to cope. If they grow up feeling unloved and unable to pay those price tags of acceptance and love, they will spend their time during adulthood trying to do one of two things, or possibly both: They struggle to win love and acceptance or to avoid pain.

I have regrouped and expanded some of Powell's examples for each of those categories. Basically, to win love and acceptance, they will become boastful and indulge in self-flattery. It's like they are waving a flag to say, "I'm somebody! Notice me! If I have to pad my resume, I will. If I have to splurge beyond my means on a bigger house or car, you will want to be around me." I remember a boy in third grade who frequently brought candy and gum from his father's store to give to kids so they would let him be in their group. He did not want to be left out during "choose up" time for softball.

If that doesn't work, the love-deprived may attempt to make you feel sorry for them by running themselves down as losers who will never amount to anything. If you do not expect much from them, then they can't be failures. Or they may become workaholics or perfectionists. They may become your personal doormat so you will notice their submissiveness. As the "all time nice person" who agrees with you on every subject, you will have to approve them.

The other side of the coin is to try to avoid pain at least. They may become the intense critic we have studied about in an earlier chapter. By directing venom toward others, one's own inadequacies are downplayed. Rationalization is employed to project blame on others and avoid responsibility for one's own actions. Anger may accompany this approach. One can become cynical and suspicious of others. It is assumed that no one else has any worth either if they have none.

Sometimes it hurts less to isolate oneself in any realm where one feels inadequate. Fear and shyness become shelters. If one becomes a timid loner who never attempts anything, then he will not fail, and it will not hurt. Refusal to engage in activity or an act of disclosure will keep others from knowing the real person who has never measured up. Sometimes hurt is diminished by surrounding oneself with things—the badges of success. Like the rich farmer in Luke 12, he may find consolation in having "much goods laid up for many years."

Sometimes the hurt is reduced by acquiring a multiple personality, to be someone else entirely. Then it will be the other person who is not accepted.

FACING REALITY

Isn't it fair, however, to say that, even if one were denied some of the benefits of healthy love while growing up, the time eventually comes when one needs to face reality and avoid gimmickry and manipulation? If one knows enough to engage in those strategies designed to win love or avoid pain, couldn't such a one also face some of the harsh realities of life? Shouldn't they eventually realize that it makes no sense to penalize innocent loved ones today, who played no part in the deprived web of life they experienced, by perpetuating a form of infantile self-pity and hurt? All of these reactions eventually bring even deeper hurt to those who are not exposed to the great love of God, the joy of forgiveness, and the genuine warm love of fellow Christians. God has revealed to the human family how to have access to the healing power of love. Love has been designed as a powerful force. Since God made humans, he knows what is needed to help them relate to him and each other successfully. Love is that drawing power that he uses.

Love is the power God uses to draw us to him.

- For God so loved the world that he gave his only begotten son, that whoever believes in him should not perish but have everlasting life (John 3:16).
- But God demonstrates his own love toward us, in that while we were still sinners, Christ died for us (Romans 5:8).
- In this the love of God was manifested toward us, that God has sent his only begotten son into the world, that we might live through him (1 John 4:9. See also v. 10).
- Love is also the power to help us meet each other's needs.
- By this we know love, because he laid down his life for us. And we also ought to lay down our lives for the brethren (1 John 3:16).
- Beloved, if God so loved us, we also ought to love one another (1 John 4:11).
- This is my commandment, that you love one another as I have loved you. Greater love has no one than this, than to lay down one's life for his friends (John 15:12-13).

You may say, "All that is well and good! But it doesn't really work that way in real life, does it?" Even good people who want to practice "Christian love" sometimes have to deal with very unlovable people! Someone has said, "Christians are people who love each other—until they are acquainted." Frankly, there are some people we just don't enjoy being around. In their presence, we prefer to be reserved and aloof. We would not want them to miss heaven, but even there, we wouldn't want to sit by them!

How is this explained? Are we running the risk of violating a cardinal part of Christ's teaching? Read again Luke 14:12-14. He said that when we plan a party, don't just invite our closest buddies that count visits with us and always pay us back. And he says to avoid the temptation to show interest only in those who can do something for us in return. He is not saying we can't have close friends or enjoy nice dinners with those whom we relate to more easily. He is saying though that at times we need to love the unlovable also. They are caught in some of these "Love Traps" we're talking about. They hurt because they get isolated. They may verbalize their hurt at times: "Nobody likes me. I might as well be dead and out of everybody's way." The more they whine and talk that way, the very traits that made them unlovable to start with are compounded and cause people to shun them even more.

WHAT MAKES ONE "UNLOVABLE?"

All of this brings up another side of the issue. Why is it that some people seem to be so unlovable? Why is it that "emotional vibes" don't seem to be flowing nicely for them? Somehow some "barriers to love" do exist. Is it all the fault of those hypocritical "do-gooder Christians" who shun them, or is there something they could identify and work on themselves to ease their hurts?

Perhaps an illustration about electrical power will help. I must admit though that I don't understand electricity that much. I don't even understand electricians! But apparently electricity is a force that flows from a transmitter to a receiver that causes some good things to happen—unless there is a short circuit! In that case, explosions or adverse effects can occur because the flow of electricity does not cause expected good results.

Now, to apply that thought: Love, as a force, flows from one person to others and is intended to cause good things to happen. Love begets love. We all seem to admit that certain qualities attract a love response, but other qualities repel a love response.

1 Corinthians 13 is the classic text in the Bible listing all the good things that are supposed to happen when love is expressed. We learn qualities of love in that chapter and freely admit that one who exhibits those qualities is lovable. May we not infer then that one who is unloved may somehow have "short-circuited" those qualities? Somehow, in the transmission process, we may have reversed the traits that successfully create a love response. We need to give ourselves a test, to see if we have created some "barriers to love" that short circuit relationships. A positive practice of 1 Corinthians 13 will win friends and bring joy. If we reverse the pro-cess, we alienate friends and get caught in the love traps that

hurt. God's plan works. If we have reversed it, the explanation for our "unloveliness" and our hurt is that simple to detect.

BARRIERS TO LOVE ERECTED BY REVERSING 1 CORINTHIANS 13

v. 1-3 "Though I speak with the tongues of men and of angels, but have not love, I have become as sounding brass or a clanging symbol. And though I have the gift of prophecy, and understand all mysteries and all knowledge, and though I have all faith, so that I could remove mountains, but have not love, I am nothing. And though I bestow all my goods to feed the poor, and though I give my body to be burned, but have not love, it profits me nothing."

Those traits should make anyone lovable. If I am not loved, here's a self-administered test: Am I too showy, phony, and pretentious? If we are not genuine, people are turned off and do not care to be around us. The sincere parent, neighbor, preacher, and friend is the most loved. Do we give people reason to question our genuineness?

v. 4a "Love suffers long ..." Am I impatient with others? Do I fail to give consideration to their feelings and demand that others make concessions to me and accept my friendship on my terms—and do it now? William Barclay referred to the early conflicts between Abraham Lincoln and Secretary Stanton. Stanton had been a hasty, harsh critic of Lincoln, calling him "the original gorilla" and "a clown." Yet Lincoln made him secretary of state because he felt he was needed. Lincoln once had sent a message to Stanton by a young man. Stanton read it and blurted out that Lincoln was a fool. Upon returning, the young man told Lincoln what Stanton had said. Lincoln said, "Perhaps Secretary Stanton is right." But Lincoln's patience eventually won. After his death, Stanton viewed his body and said, "There lies the greatest leader of men the world has known."

v. 4b "Love is kind ..." If our loving relationships with others have been short-circuited, is it because we are harsh and rigidly unpleasant to be around? Are we abrupt with others and cruelly cold? We have a saying that "you can catch more flies with honey than you can with vinegar." We may need to "sweeten up" in the way we come across to people.

v. 4c "Love does not envy ..." Envy has been defined as "Pain felt and malignity conceived at the sight of excellence on the part of another." Do we hurt, or feel pain, because we envy others? Are we jealous? Do we begrudge others the success they have in life? According to James 3:14–18, envy and jealousy are sins. Sometimes a grossly immoral person whose sins are openly observed might be publicly disciplined, whereas a jealous, envious bully could tyrannize a congregation and cause hurt for years without notice.

v.4d "Love does not parade itself ..." Are we braggarts? Boastful? Arrogant? Truly great, lovable people are humble and unassuming, never putting others down. As one has said, "Only one person has the right to boast and that's the man who never does." There is a story of two men who went to a railroad station in a small town to buy a ticket. The agent was very uppity and insulting. After transacting the purchase, one of the men said, "I never knew it to fail—the littler the station, the bigger the agent!"

v. 4e "(Love) is not puffed up ..." Maybe we need to ask ourselves if we are unduly inflated with our own importance? Others will sense it and distance themselves from us. Am I conceited? Has success gone to my head? Am I too good to do my part? Is it beneath my dignity to serve others?

There is a story about Albert Schweitzer, whose name was synonymous with service to others. Regardless of what we know or think about his personal beliefs, we admire a person who will sacrifice his life in service to a humanitarian cause. Once while he was struggling to put a piece of lumber in place to build an addition to his hospital, he asked a young native who was watching to help him. The young man replied, "Sir, I have been to school. I am an intellectual. I do not have to do work like that anymore." Meanwhile, one of the world's truly great intellectuals was performing a menial task.

I thought of this when I went to Bangladesh to teach one fall. In the airport, I met a young native of Nepal who was returning home after being in the USA to go to Harvard. As we sat on the plane, I asked several questions about his country. I said, "I'm sure it will be very rewarding to you to return home and use your talents to help your people enjoy a higher standard of living." I noticed that his response was rather noncommittal and that he changed the subject. I did not pursue it further and neither did he. It did not dawn on me why he seemed so evasive to discuss the subject until I picked up a small book about Nepal two weeks later. The book about the country described in detail that a strong motivation for the young people there was to get a higher education so they could be liberated from menial service. Once educated, they would be spared the task of community service. That was the chore of the illiterate!

v. 5a (Love) does not behave itself rudely (unseemly) .... So: Am I blunt? Tactless? Boorish? Rude? Impolite? Discourteous? Peter exhorted early Christians to "have compassion one for another, love as brothers, be tenderhearted, be courteous" (1 Peter 3:8).

Josh Billings once said, "One of the greatest victories you can gain over a man is to beat him at politeness." That was illustrated once in a decision President McKinley made when he began his term as President of the United States. He had narrowed his choices to two men for an important post. They seemed to be on equal footing for the appointment—until the President remembered an incident he had observed on a streetcar some years before. Before McKinley was President, he once got on a car late at night and took the only vacant seat. An elderly woman carrying a heavy basket of clothes got on at the next stop. One of those men, he remembered, was sitting near the woman, but he shifted his newspaper so he would not see her. Instead, McKinley got up and invited the woman to come take his seat. When the President remembered how that man had been purposely impolite, he chose the other man for the post. The man never knew how his small act of unkindness cost him a promotion he would have liked to have very much.

v.5b (Love) "does not seek its own ..." So: Am I selfish? Do I look out for "number one" to have my rights, regardless of others? Is there a sort of ruthless disregard for the rights of others due to an exaggerated sense of my own importance?

A woman barged in front of a long line ahead of her at a checkout counter and blurted, "I'm in a hurry and need a can of cat food! Can you get me one now, please!" While the inexperienced clerk complied, the woman sensed some hostility when she looked at the line of stunned people. Then she said, "I'm really in a hurry. I hope you don't mind that I went ahead of you for just one item." One of them answered, "Not if you're that hungry, dearie!"

Perhaps we all recognize the occasional unavoidable emergency and hope others will understand, but the self-centered demands of the self-appointed VIP is another matter—and always alienates.

v. 5c Love "is not provoked" So: Am I quick to fly into a temper outburst? Am I temperamental and high strung? Do I show exasperation quickly and impulsively? Those are not only traits that make others keep their distance from us; they violate directly some Biblical commands: "Let every man be swift to hear, slow to speak, slow to wrath, for the wrath of man does not produce the righteousness of God" (James 1:19–20). And also, there is Proverbs 14:29: "He who is slow to wrath has great understanding, but he who is impulsive, exalts folly."

v. 5d Love "thinks no evil." So: Do I "chalk up wrongs?" Am I suspicious? Do I carry grudges? Do I nurse wrath? Am I accusatory, always assuming the worst rather than giving the benefit of the doubt? If we do not know the full facts, even when we see a situation that on the surface looks a bit suspicious, if we love another, we will interpret the matter a hundred different ways before we conclude the worst. A lot of families have had serious misunderstandings, sometimes that led to violence, when an overactive imagination thought the worst! Maybe not all cases were as severe as that of a man who came home late one night. The next day, a co-worker asked how things went. He said, "It was awful. My wife got historical last night, and we had a dispute that went for hours."

His friend said, "You mean she got hysterical, don't you?" He said, "No, I mean historical. She brought up every mistake I've made during the whole time we've been married."

He may still have fared better than the man who entered the wrong house and was beaten up by a woman before she realized he was not her husband. She was very apologetic when she realized her mistake, but he said, "That's no use! I'll still have to go through the same or worse when I get to my house!" People who love each other have to find better ways to interpret how the other acts.

v. 6a Love "does not rejoice in iniquity." So: Do I get pleasure out of the wrongs of others? Am I happy when others stumble? Am I an open-eared gossiper who gets my kicks out of being a vulture who likes to hear and pass on the worst about others? There are people who seem to rejoice in the morbid and the shortcomings of others. One lady once said, as if with disappointment, "There were no interesting deaths today."

Someone has said that "Muckraking, mudslinging books about the sins of good men are more popular than biographies of the saints' lives." I knew a lady once who said to her husband, "I just wish you would have an affair so I could have a scriptural right to get rid of you!" Presumably, she would have rejoiced in hearing of any such iniquity on his part.

v. 6b Love "rejoices in the truth." So: Am I prejudiced? Am I unyielding and strongly opinionated? Even if I am wrong, would I rather no one tell me or expect me to make a correction? This should impress on us the depth of the love many have had for God's truth when they have made painful decisions to make changes in their religious practices, even at the expense of being alienated from families and religious traditions that have been previously dear to them, in order to serve God simply as New Testament Christians.

v. 7a Love "bears all things ..." So: Am I unable to endure anything that requires patience? Am I undependable? Am I a quitter? Am I more comfortable to be a loser who gives up without finishing any challenging task?

A stone cutter hammers away at a huge rock, blow after blow without cracking it. Eventually one blow splits it into two pieces. He knows it was not that last blow that did it. It was the compounded effect of all that went before that last blow. The world often unfairly idolizes the "hero" who had one flash of instant glory merely by coincidence, instead of showing appreciation for the patient caregiver who bears a lifetime of duty doing unpleasant chores the "hero" would not even dare to tackle. Thank God for Heaven and the promise that someday all these injustices can be rectified.

v. 7b Love "believes all things ..." So: Am I distrustful? Do I alienate others by communicating bluntly that I have no faith or confidence in them? Young people don't seem to understand this nature of love. Sometimes I try to tell them that "it takes more than love to make a marriage work. It takes respect." It's all borne out in Ephesians 5. Loss of respect can kill love, so more than love is necessary. Respect keeps the trust alive; without it, a marriage can die.

Someone has said, "There's only one thing finer than to have a friend you can trust, and that is to have a friend who will trust you."

v. 7c Love "hopes all things ..." So: Am I a four-star pessimist? Do I always see the bad side and never the good side? Do I quickly lose hope and dash the optimism and dreams of all who are around me?

A preacher was going to visit a lady who was a confirmed pessimist. In the past, he had been to see her and always left feeling that her negative outlook was contagious. On this day, he decided he was going to beat her to the draw. He was going to lock her in to an optimistic reaction. He said, "My, isn't this a beautiful day! We certainly can't find any fault with one like this can we?" She said, "Yes, but just think what it'll be like tomorrow!" I thought of the youth who liked to visit a nursing home and play the piano for the residents. She said, "What would you like for me to play for you?" One of them said, "It really doesn't matter, just so it's sad." It really is sad to lose all hope.

v. 7d and 8a "Love endures all things ... Love never fails ..." So: Am I fickle? Do I wilt without fortitude at the first sign of an obstacle? Do I show no grit, no active persistence even to try to bear unpleasant things?

We must realize that no normal person that we think we would like to be around is going to set his/her alarm clock to rise early and rush into the presence of whining, complaining people who give up on life without trying, while blaming everyone else at the same time for their troubles.

CONCLUSION

If you will go back and construct a composite of the personality of the person who has reversed all these traits of love in his or her life, you should be able to see a profile that unlocks a puzzle for you. The person who is hurting might be able to remove some of these barriers to love.

It has been said that "He who has love in his heart has spurs in his sides." We have studied God's plan for a better world. Love, properly defined and practiced, will bring great joy and happiness to the world. Do you love God? Do you love yourself? Do you love others whom God also loves? Love for God is rather easily proved.

Jesus said, "If you love me, you will keep my commandments." It should not be difficult to return love to one who loved us first.

QUESTIONS FOR DISCUSSION

1. As an overview of this lesson, what would you offer as a good working definition of love?
2. Does everyone have an equal appetite for love?
3. What do you think accounts for the fact that some individuals are less inclined to show their affections?
4. Without dealing directly in personalities, can you give any examples of individuals as adults who seek either to gain acceptance or avoid pain due to the circumstances they experienced in earlier life?
5. Identify and discuss some things that young parents should be doing now to insure that their children feel loved and accepted in their respective homes.
6. Comment on the various "barriers to love" that were mentioned in the lesson. Can you think of additional ways to expand on any of them?
7. Discuss the possibility of trust and love being cultivated again after earlier experiences that may have "killed it." What types of things might work to ease the hurt?

8. What could help each of us to grow in our love for God and Christ? What can be done among Christians to help "brotherly love continue," as we are commanded in Hebrews 13:1?

6

THE LIMITS OF LOVE
BILL BAGENTS

Likely, you've heard the following statements in one form or another:

- Love conquers all.
- There's nothing love can't do.
- Love will find a way.
- All we need is love.
- Love is the greatest power in the universe.
- Love never fails.

"Love never fails" carries more weight than the others. You recognize it as a direct quote from 1 Corinthians 13:8. Like the others, it seems to imply that love always ensures the very best outcome. Love never disappoints. Love never lets anyone down. Not only that, it seems to imply that the power of love can keep those whom we love from letting us (or God) down.

THE LIMITS OF LOVE

Such thinking is dangerous and unbiblical. It is a prelude to pain.

The longer I live, the more I am certain of the truth of every word of Scripture. At the same time, the longer I live, the more I realize that understanding Scripture is hard work. It's so easy to think that the first sentence of 1 Corinthians 13:8 says more than it really says.

Many translators render the phrase in question, "Love never ends." One paraphrase reads, "Love is eternal." Another says, "Love goes on forever." I am persuaded that this is the most accurate understanding of the unfailing nature of love. Check the context for yourself! You'll see that it "fits."

You may be wondering, "Why is he bothering us with this technical discussion?" Good question! You may have noticed that when it comes to the subject of easing life's hurts, I tend to focus on prevention. I think of prevention as "healing in advance." Our current subject, "The Limits of Love," is an attempt to describe one of the most pervasive and insidious "Love Traps." That "trap" is the snare of believing that those we love will always do right if we just love them enough. In truth, we can save ourselves considerable pain by realizing that love has limits.

EXAMPLES FROM SCRIPTURE

Who could doubt God's love for His chosen people? It took a miracle to give Abraham and Sarah a son. It took God's guiding hand to preserve Isaac's descendants through seven years of famine. It took a series of mighty acts to free His people from bondage in Egypt and to give them the promised land.

His chosen people were the Lord's beloved. They were blessed with leaders like Moses and David, with prophets like Isaiah and Jeremiah, and with the precious law of God. Please note the parable recorded in Isaiah 5:1–7. The Lord asks, "What more could have been done to My vineyard that I have not done in it?" Despite God's care and love, His people forsook Him.

No one could doubt David's love for Absalom, his son. The murder of Amnon was forgiven. It took some doing, but after a time of exile, Absalom was finally back home (2 Samuel 13–14).

When their reunion was complete, David kissed his son (2 Samuel 14:33).

Absalom repaid his father with rebellion. Rebellion led to civil war. But as wrong as Absalom was, David still loved him. We remember the king's orders just before the final battle: "Deal gently for my sake with the young man Absalom" (2 Samuel 18:5). Even David's grief at the death of his son shows the depth of his love (2 Samuel 18:33). He would gladly have died for the boy, but even that love could not change Absalom's heart.

There can be no doubt that Jesus loved the man whom we call "the rich young ruler." Mark 10:21 begins, "Then, Jesus looking at him loved him..." In that Jesus is our perfect example, I think of Jesus loving this man with a perfect love. The Lord loved him to show him compassion and to tell him the truth. Still, the man "was sad at this word, and went away grieved ..." (Mark 10:21). Even the love of Jesus could not move him to obedience!

THE LIMITS OF LOVE

We know the love that Jesus has for every soul. John the Baptizer's statement of that love is recorded in John 1:29: "Behold! The Lamb of God who takes away the sins of the world!" Jesus Himself stated, "I am the living bread which came down from heaven. If anyone eats of this bread, he will live forever; and the bread that I shall give is My flesh which I shall give for the life of the world" (John 6:51). John 10:11 records the more familiar statement, "I am the good shepherd. The good shepherd gives His life for the sheep."

Though the love of God led the Father to send His Son and the love of Jesus led Him from heaven to the cross, the majority of humanity refuses to respond to their love. Many walk the broad way, but few walk the "strait and narrow" (Matthew 7:13–14). There are limits, even to the love of God.

We offer one final example from Scripture. Romans 9:1–5 is one of the saddest paragraphs in all the Bible. Paul loved his countrymen. Their rejection of Jesus led him to "great sorrow and continual grief" of heart. His love was so strong that he could write, "For I could wish that I myself were accursed from Christ for my brethren, my kinsmen according to the flesh…"

As great as it was, Paul's love could not move the majority of his countrymen to saving faith in Christ. It was not for lack of intensity. It was not for lack of effort. It's just that, as strong as love is, there are limits to the power of love.

DIFFICULT TRUTH

Why is it so often so difficult to face the fact that love has limits? When our thinking is at its best, we all recognize this truth. Perhaps that is one answer: our thinking isn't always at its best. Sometimes, we "think" with our hearts more than with our heads. Sometimes we let our feelings overrule our thinking. If we're not very careful, we can even be tempted to let our feelings "tell" us more than is true.

Consider the "make believe" example of Amy and Joe. They've been dating for more than a year. The wedding date is set. Amy is a Christian, but Joe isn't. He has so many wonderful qualities and a few that aren't so wonderful. First, there's the fact that he's living without Jesus. He has a bit too much temper. And, he lacks the measure of tenderness that Amy wants and needs.

Amy's parents see these "flaws" much more clearly than Amy does. The same is true of her friends. But Amy isn't worried. She trusts the power of love. She'll marry Joe and help him change. Surely, he'll change. After all, he loves her.

Jack Wilhelm tells a story he remembered hearing Willard Collins tell many years ago. As the bride walks in on her wedding day, the first thing she sees is the aisle. Her second sight is the altar. And her third sight is the groom. Naturally, all the way down to take his hand, she's thinking, "Aisle. Altar. Him."

Amy could be right. Joe could change. But we know that there are no guarantees. Joe will change only if he chooses to change. [The sad truth is that there seem to be ten "Joes" who don't change for everyone who does.] No matter how much Amy loves him, she can't make him change. If she tries to make him, sparks are sure to fly! No matter how much we love them, we cannot make others change.

It is sometimes hard to admit that love has limits because facing that fact can look like we're giving up. Giving up is un-American. Giving up is un-Christian. Giving up goes against the core of our being.

It is not my purpose to advocate giving up. My purpose is to help us spare ourselves needless pain. There's a tremendous and vital difference between giving up and recognizing the limits of love.

I love the parable of the prodigal son (Luke 15:11–32). We know that his father loved him. He gave his son the "early inheritance" that he requested. We imagine his tears as his son left home. We imagine this father looking longingly down the road each day, hoping to see his son returning home. We know his reaction of love and compassion when the boy finally did return.

Many teachers have asked of this parable, "Why did the father let him go?" I believe the most reasonable answer is, "Because he couldn't stop him." Others ask, "Why didn't the father go after him?" I like to think that the father knew the limits of love. He knew that it was not within his power to bring the boy home. The best he could do was to wait, pray, and hope. I like to think that this father knew that he didn't cause the separation. There was no lack of love in his heart. The lack of love belonged to his son. Love demanded that the father wait for his son to make that discovery.

It can be difficult to recognize the limits of love because love is so powerful. Love made the seven years which Jacob worked for the privilege of marrying Rachel seem like just a few days (Genesis 29:20). Love made Ruth leave both her homeland and the religion of her youth (Ruth 1:15–18). Love led God the Father to send His only Son into a world filled with His enemies (Romans 5:6–11).

We have seen love melt hearts which seemed to be made of stone. We have seen love heal wounds which seemed to be permanent. We have seen love accomplish what neither fear nor force could ever hope to achieve. It's easy to see why we resist surrendering the illusion that love conquers all.

First Corinthians 13 tells us the truth. Love is patient and kind. Love sustains, hopes, and endures. Yet, we know that Matthew 23:37 is just as true. The Lord said, "O Jerusalem, Jerusalem, the one who kills the prophets and stones those who are sent to her! How often I wanted to gather your children together, as a hen gathers her chicks under her wings, but you were not willing!" What a statement! Even the power of the Lord's perfect love could not overcome their unwillingness.

True to its nature, Scripture shows such balance and wisdom in teaching on this point. The very same passage which commands, "Let love be without hypocrisy ... Be kindly affectionate to one another with brotherly love;" also commands, "Bless those who persecute you; bless and do not curse ... Repay no one evil for evil" (Romans 12:9–21). Not everyone will respond favorably, even to the most Christ-like love.

THE LIMITS OF LOVE

It can be difficult to acknowledge the limits of love because doing so often forces us to wait. We don't like to wait, especially for things we count important. We're certain that the father of the prodigal son neither wanted to wait nor enjoyed waiting for his son to "come to himself." He waited, because in a world of free moral choice, he had no better choice.

We think of the faithful wives who are described in 1 Peter 3:1–6. We know that these Christian ladies wanted their husbands to join them in obedience to Christ. It seems natural to think of them encouraging their spouses day after day. Peter gently reminded these godly women that it might not be words which could win their husbands. It might be their consistent Christian examples which carried the day.

Waiting for love to move others to action is difficult for many reasons. It forces us to realize that we are not in control. It tries our patience. It tries our faith. At the same time, waiting is often good for us. It reminds us that God is in control. It reminds us that we are often shortsighted and lack perspective. It reminds us that only God is utterly faithful and trustworthy. It pushes us toward passages like Isaiah 40:27–31 and Psalm 46. In short, it builds wisdom, patience, and faith.

It can be difficult to admit the limits of love because doing so forces us to acknowledge that we are not in control. Of course, I'm not denying that we are both free to choose our actions and responsible before God for the actions that we choose. The reminder is that we are not in control of the universe. We aren't even in control of the actions of those we love most.

It is heartbreaking to talk with parents who are telling themselves, "Our child would never have done these terrible things if we had just loved him more." It's just as sad to hear a godly lady say, "My husband is such a good person. I know he'd be a Christian now if I had just loved him more."

Wanting to abound in love is a noble virtue (1 Thessalonians 4:9–10). Our love should be growing in both quantity and quality (Romans 12:9–21, 1 Corinthians 13, Philippians 2:1–11). But if the love of Christ was not enough to save Judas or the rich young ruler, then we cannot rightly fault ourselves when our love is either rejected or ignored. The guilt we feel in such cases is a false guilt. A vital part of easing this hurt is reminding ourselves that we did not cause it. We must fight the hurt that comes from situations which we did not cause and could not prevent.

WHAT'S THE BIG DEAL?

What happens when people fail to recognize the limits of love? We have just discussed the devastating consequence of false guilt. Sadly, there are many other highly damaging effects.

Those who don't admit that love has limits often face the merry-go-round complex. They believe that everything will be perfect if they can just make things "spin a little faster." If only they can do a few more loving things or say a few more loving words or provide a few more loving dollars, then they are sure to see the desired results. I believe that I have seen people fall to exhaustion still believing that they could make things right if only they could do just a little more.

Those who don't acknowledge the limits of love don't always fall to exhaustion. Sometimes they fall to denial. Being unable to do enough to make everything right, they choose to pretend that everything is perfect.

Such denial exacts a terrible price. It often makes others see us as dishonest, as unwilling to face the truth. It makes us think less of ourselves. Denial and guilt are frequent companions. It sometimes even manifests itself in physical illness. The Lord made us to be truthful. Dishonesty, in any form, always takes a toll.

Others who don't admit that love has limits become clingers. They "grab hold and hold on for dear life." It's as if they believe that any distance or space within their relationships will cause them to collapse.

In truth, every healthy relationship involves both closeness and distance, both togetherness and space. Relationships become smothering when we forget that fact. Love does not mean that we have no time apart, no differences of opinion, and no other friendships. Mature love doesn't smother. It doesn't seek to control. Mature love frees us to enjoy greater quality in all our friendships. We have saved the worst for last—false guilt. If I had to list only one terrible cost of refusing to recognize the limits of love, it would be false guilt. False guilt is guilt over things that we have no power to change. It is guilt over situations that are beyond our control. It is guilt over the bad choices which others make against our will and despite our prayers.

False guilt feels just like legitimate guilt. The pain is

just as real and just as deep. What makes it false is the lack of culpability on our part. We didn't cause it. More likely, we did all we could to prevent it.

We must reject false guilt. That is a vital aspect of easing life's hurts. Think of Jesus in the example we mentioned above from Matthew 23:37. There's pain in His words, but it's not the pain of guilt. It's the pain of rejection. Knowing the difference is crucial to our emotional and spiritual well-being. Even the Lord's love could not change those who rejected it. While that truth still hurts, at least it's an honest hurt. It's the kind of pain which God can use to build our character and draw us closer to Him.

QUESTIONS FOR DISCUSSION

1. Why do so many people seem to believe that there are no limits to the power of love?
2. What are your favorite biblical examples of the power of love?
3. How can recognizing the limits of the power of love help protect us from life's hurts?
4. In what settings or relationships is it especially tempting to forget that even love has limits?
5. Is it really true that believing there are no limits to the power of love is "a prelude to pain"? Explain.
6. What wise (and sometimes difficult) actions

might recognizing the limits of love cause us to take?
7. Is false guilt as damaging as this lesson describes it to be? Give reasons for your answer.

7

THE HURTS CAUSED BY OTHERS
JACK P. WILHELM

The world has never had a shortage of evildoers. The Bible refers to them frequently. Sometimes they are called workers of iniquity, wicked ones, and followers of an evil way.

W. E. Vine uses the following terms to describe evildoers: "What is evil in character, effect, influence ... what is destructive, injurious, ... pernicious ... causes pain, sorrow, malignant evil ... belonging to a low order of things ... denotes wickedness, depravity, malignity ... to do harm." They certainly qualify to be included in a list of things we have to contend with that cause hurts in life.

The term evildoer is used at least 17 times in the King James Version of the Bible, most in the Psalms (e.g. in 26:5, 37:1,9, 94:16, and 119:115). But Christians were warned about them, also, especially in 1 Peter 2:12, 14, 3:16, and 4:15.

NO SHORTAGE OF EVILDOERS TODAY

We would like to think that all evildoers lived only in the ancient past and that the world that has benefited by the elevating influence of the gospel could be spared the uncivilized hurts of the ancient world. But evildoers are not an extinct species! The daily newspaper records how they are at work daily:

• Crime reports indicate that our chances of being a victim increase regularly. Many cities are now unsafe for people to be out at night—and even in the daytime in some places. The sale of security devices, locks, alarm systems, watch dogs, and guns is big business.

• The news media tell of elderly people cowering in fear indoors, fearful that hoodlums will break in on them to rob them. Sometimes senseless vandalism and destruction of property cause extra worry and expense for all neighborhoods.

• On a larger scale, some entire small countries and races of people have been caused extensive hurt by warlords, terrorists, and power-hungry despots. People in Rwanda, Somalia, Indonesia, Ireland, Kosovo, northern Iraq, Croatia, Tibet, and Korea, as starters, can tell you what it is like to be victims of evildoers. There are some places in the United States where victims can tell you also!

• Sometimes, streaks of meanness also show up in ordinarily "good people." Confidences built up over years get shattered. Deep hurts are inflicted because Christian principles mean little to a growing cadre of punks and rebels. But sometimes, the innocent are victimized by religious people. Remember that the early church suffered most in its early days by persecutors like Saul of Tarsus who was feared because of "the much harm that he has done" (Acts 9:13). Yet he was just having fun with people he disagreed with in religion.

Someone said, "If you want to know the true character of a person, watch what he does to his neighbor in the name of religion." Some of the greatest tragedies in history were perpetrated by religious people, including the ones who caused the crucifixion of Jesus Christ. Saul of Tarsus, who persecuted the Christians so severely, was a very religious person.

"DO NOT FRET BECAUSE OF EVILDOERS"

The book of Psalms contains many references to the distress God's people felt because of the bullies of the world. Psalm 58:1–6 is a good example. The verses speak of the violence in the earth caused by "the wicked who are estranged from the womb. They go astray as soon as they are born, speaking lies!" In despair, the Psalmist cried out, "Break their teeth, o God, in their mouth!" See also Psalm 78:1–7.

That sentiment seems strangely up to date in a prayer that someone has compiled, hopefully facetiously:

"May those who love us, always love us!

And, if they do not love us, may they change their hearts!

And, if they do not change their hearts, then may they turn their ankles—so we can know them by their limp!"

God's people were told in Psalm 37:1 not to fret because of evildoers. What would tempt us to fret and feel hurt because of them?

Sometimes we may feel hurt because we fear that evildoers will harm us. It seems normal for us to fear bodily harm, because some of God's most courageous servants of the past did so. At least twice, Abraham was fearful that he might be killed so that his wife could be taken from him (Genesis 12:13 and 20:11). The pattern was repeated in Genesis 26:7 by his son Isaac. David's fears led him to commit grievous sins and cover-ups (2 Samuel 11, 12), and Peter also denied the Lord out of fear (John 18:15-18).

The wisdom of Proverbs is needed to ease these hurts: "The fear of man brings a snare, but whoever trusts in the Lord shall be safe" (29:25). Jesus taught that his disciples should not fear those who can kill the body but do no more harm; rather they were to fear God who could destroy both soul and body (Matthew 10:28).

Sometimes we may feel hurt because we envy the evildoer. Sometimes Christians bristle at God's "thou shalt nots." We feel that we are missing out on all the fun! Preachers have actually heard such statements as these: "Don't preach to me about what I need to do. I know as well as you do, but I'm not getting any younger and life is passing me by. I think I'm entitled to some fun. Others seem to be doing these things and getting by without any penalty. Why can't I?" Ecclesiastes 8:11-13 is as modern as tomorrow's newspaper in describing this mindset:

Because the sentence against an evil work is not

executed speedily, therefore the heart of the sons of men is fully set in them to do evil. Though a sinner does evil a hundred times, and his days are prolonged, yet I surely know that it will be well with those who fear God, who fear before him. But it will not be well with the wicked.

Sometimes the rebels add, "We only go around once! There ought to be some way that Christians can enjoy pleasures without having guilt heaped on them!" The mindset of feeling "left out" must have been a problem to the people of the Old Testament because the same passage in Psalm 37 that told God's people not to fret because of evildoers told them in the next verse not to envy them! Do you remember that the book of Proverbs contained many wise exhortations of a father to his son to get wisdom and avoid being reckless? Part of that wisdom was contained in this warning: "Do not fret because of evildoers, nor be envious of the wicked, for there will be no prospect for the evil man; the lamp of the wicked will be put out! Do not associate with those given to change; for their calamity will rise suddenly, and who knows the ruin those two can bring" (Proverbs 24:19–22).

AN OLD PROBLEM: WHY DO THE WICKED PROSPER?

Sometimes we are made uncomfortable by observing the apparent prosperity of the wicked. If so, read carefully and slowly Psalm 73. It will do much to ease the hurt of those envious feelings. Let verses 2 and 16–19 serve as "bookend verses" to those in between them. Notice that the Psalmist said, "When I thought how to understand this, it was too painful for me...!" (v. 16) Sometimes we just don't understand how the wicked seem to prosper. It is painful. But the full story of God's care for his people will ease that hurt for us today as it did those first readers centuries ago!

HOW TO AVOID FRETTING BECAUSE OF EVILDOERS

The thirty-seventh Psalm contains an ancient remedy for the modern ills of coping with the evildoer problem. Look at how practical it is:

We need to remember that God is still in command. We need to remain convinced of God's power and concern. Notice how that idea is contained in several of the verses in Psalm 37. "Rest in the Lord, and wait patiently for him," v. 7. In verses 23–24, the Psalmist said, "The steps of a good man are ordered by the Lord, and he delights in his way. Though he fall, he shall not be utterly cast down; for the Lord upholds him with his hand." These thoughts were built upon the premise already laid down in verses 12–13: "The wicked plots against the just, and gnashes at him with his teeth. The Lord laughs at him, for he sees that his day is coming."

There is the additional assurance of verses 17 and 18: "The Lord upholds the righteous," and "the Lord knows the days of the upright."

Almost anywhere one reads in this chapter, there are references to the greatness and power of God. It's the same in other books of the Bible. For example, in Revelation, the Sovereignty of God was established in chapter 4 before the description of coming persecution was given, to assure the faithful that God was still in charge and they would eventually be victorious.

Somehow, we need to restore our childlike faith in God's omnipresence and power. A mother saw her little son scratching in the Bible. She rebuked him for treating the Bible that way. Then she learned that he had been reading Mark 9:22 where one approached Jesus with a problem and said, "If you can do anything, have compassion on us and help us." The little boy said, "I don't think the man should have said 'IF,' so I'm scratching that word out." With God, in the matter of caring for his people who are victims of evildoers, it is not a matter of IF but only a matter of WHEN.

We need to direct our minds to higher goals that are compatible with God's goals for us. In verse 4 of Psalm 37, we read, "Delight yourself also in the Lord, and he shall give you the desires of your heart." A word of caution: This verse has been misused by some who want it to be a blank check to provide them with selfish, misdirected wants.

I knew an old preacher once who botched a lot of Bible teaching—and who seemed to enjoy handling the word recklessly! One day on his radio program, he declared arrogantly, "I ain't sick today and I won't be sick tomorrow!" Somebody asked him how he could justify such a conclusion. He said, "Because the Bible says God will give us the desires of our heart and I don't desire to be sick tomorrow." However, he died not long after that, so we can assume God either didn't keep his word or the old gentleman changed the "*dezarr* of his heart" as he called it. Obviously, he was committing God to a position he had not made, although it is true that things will go better for us as we turn our requests over to God and seek the higher goals that are compatible with doing his will.

Regarding our desires, we are asked to exercise our minds to discern good from evil (Hebrews 5:12-14). Also, we are taught to set our affections on things above (Colossians 3:1-2). Doing this will position us to cope with the evildoers better. But if it takes our being victimized by some evildoer to make us re-evaluate our goals and be more submissive, spiritual, and prayerful, can we say that it has been a totally bad experience? Many who are scarred by some evildoer have a much deeper perspective of what life is all about than they otherwise would have. From Psalm 37 we learn also to occupy ourselves in doing positive deeds of service to others. Notice in verse 3 that in addition to trusting in the Lord, we are asked to "do good." This was the method Jesus used: "God anointed Jesus of Nazareth with the Holy Spirit and with power, who went about doing good ..." (Acts 10:38). This was also the method Jesus taught his disciples to use: "He who finds his life will lose it, and he who loses his life for my sake will find it" (Matthew 10:39).

One way to cope with evildoers in this connection was mentioned by Peter in 1 Peter 2:12. He realized that some slanderous critics might even call the Christians evildoers. If that were to happen, he said that if Christians conduct themselves honorably, "When they speak against you as evildoers, they may, by your good works which they observe, glorify God in the day of visitation." This recipe is compatible with other admonitions given to Christians, such as those in Galatians 6:10 and James 1:27. When one has done and given his best in service to the Lord, he will not have the regrets that one has who holds back on doing good when opportunity presents itself.

It was told once that Queen Mary took a walk in Scotland when a quick shower came up unexpectedly. The Queen's attendants approached a local resident to borrow an umbrella. The person did not recognize the Queen, so she loaned a spare umbrella from her attic that had a broken rib and some holes in it. She did not want to risk loaning a better umbrella, lest she not get it back. When the Queen returned the old umbrella the next day, she sent it with a note on royal stationery, expressing her thanks. The owner regretted deeply not having loaned her best to the Queen after realizing her missed opportunity.

Maybe there's another side to this that explains why we let our caution make us reluctant to put ourselves out. I remember once when a passerby stopped at the church office asking for a handout. Churches located near the highways get a lot of those and we get calloused, realizing that some people don't try to help themselves and exploit the good nature of church people. She looked the part well—disheveled, battle scarred, and demanding. I explained that we didn't keep cash at the office and that we would need to do some checking to see how we could help. She explained, "But

I've not eaten in two days. Surely you could arrange for us to get something to eat!"

I said, "Well, I've brought my lunch today which I will be glad to let you have. I can skip my lunch and get something to eat later."

She said, "I don't know. What is it?"

I said, "I think it's a tuna fish sandwich."

Indignantly, she said, "I couldn't eat anything that junky! We'll just go on!" Whereupon she left, apparently not nearly as hungry as she had first declared. Which meant I got to eat the junky stuff after all!

It is true that sometimes, no matter how good our intentions are, there will be limitations to the good we can do. But we can make the offer in good faith, while avoiding being reckless and fool hardy. After all, Jesus told us to be "wise as serpents and as harmless as doves" (Matthew 10:16). There is a time and place for caution.

We need to submit ourselves in total commitment to God and his will for us. Verse 5 of Psalm 37 called on us to "Commit your way to the Lord; trust also in him and he will bring it to pass." The expression total commitment has been done an injustice. It has been warped by mind controllers and cultic manipulators who "seek to exercise dominion over you." Jesus expressly declared that those tactics were not to be used among his disciples, (Matthew 20:25–28). The concept of total commitment is good if it is used in reference to healthy voluntary service in submission to the lordship of Christ. Jesus has been made "both Lord and Christ" and we are to accept him fully as such (Acts 2:36–40; Philippians 2:5–11). The Samaritans, the eunuch, and Saul of

Tarsus model such yielding for us to God's will (Acts 8 and 9).

Commitment is designed to end indecision for us. Once indecision is ended, we can cope with the opposition of the evil doers and even turn their confrontations into opportunities that make us grow. Paul viewed his imprisonment by evildoers as a positive opportunity to further the gospel (Philippians 1:12ff). A favorite illustration of ministers involves the oyster and the grains of sand that irritate it. A grain of sand, as a foreign object, causes pain to the oyster. It tries to eject it if it can. If it cannot, the oyster excretes a substance that insulates the grain of sand to reduce the discomfort. In time, the continuing excretion hardens and becomes a priceless pearl. The oyster did not consciously intend to manufacture a pearl. It could not care less about it. It is merely trying to ease its hurt. But beauty emerged from its pain because it chose an alternate route to compensate for its problem.

Our problem is that we sometimes try to ignore God's plan, or restructure it, instead of being fully submissive. That may well defeat the purpose for what God wants us to learn. A missionary once sent some natives a sundial as a gift to show appreciation for their kindness. It never worked for them because they erected a shelter over it to cover their treasured gift! Romans 8:28 is still part of God's word.

A final suggestion emerges from Psalm 37: If we want to cope successfully with the evildoers, we must learn to be patient. "Rest in the Lord and wait patiently for him; do not fret because of him who prospers in his way ... do not fret, it only causes harm!" (Psalm 37:7–8) We are reminded that in God's own time, "Evildoers shall be cut off; but those who wait on the Lord–they shall inherit the earth. For yet a little while and the wicked shall be no more ..." (Psalm 37:9–10).

Later in the chapter, the Psalmist exhorts: "Wait on the Lord, and keep his way, and he shall exalt you to inherit the land. When the wicked are cut off, you shall see it" (v. 34).

God does not punch a time clock. He is not in a hurry. But there has never been a time that, given enough time, right has not prevailed and truth has not come to light with the wicked reaping what they sow. Patience is the key to the power to survive and surpass.

CONCLUSION

We must continue to trust God to do the right thing. He is still in control. His laws are still at work. If we will do our part and be patiently submissive to him, we will be able to see that his unchanging principles of truth are still trustworthy. If we feel that our hurts are not eased and something is still not working right, it may be that we still need to make some adjustments or view things from another angle.

There is a story about the naturalist Richard Jeffries, who spent much of his time studying the heavens and the stars. One night, as he sat by a window, waiting, for his favorite star to appear darkness came. Other stars of lesser magnitude and interest to him appeared, but he did not see the favorite he was looking for. Suddenly a puff of wind caused a leaf on a nearby tree to move. There it was, where it had been all the time! It had been temporarily hidden by such a minute, fragile thing as one leaf!

God undergirds us all the time. It may be our limited vision that clouds the view, or some distraction that for the moment means more to us. Perhaps it is time that we looked more closely at our personal relationship to God.

QUESTIONS FOR DISCUSSION

1. What have you found to be helpful to say to those who feel that once they become Christians, they should never have any other hurts in life?
2. What comes to your mind when you hear or read the word evildoer? Do you think there are fewer or more really evil people in the world today than in the past?
3. What are some of the specific fears that you know about that prompt people to take expensive and extensive measures to secure their property? What are some of the measures that may be effective for physical security?
4. What are some effective means we should be employing to rear our children so they will not envy the prosperous and glamorous image of wicked people of the world?

5. What would you say to people who are frustrated for "missing out on all the fun" and might be willing to make foolish decisions that might be costly to them in loss of family or career?
6. What do you think total commitment to God calls on one to do? Is it a Biblical concept? Has it been abused?
7. To what degree should Christians exercise caution in responding to opportunities to do good to others? When are dangers involved that might justify not getting involved?
8. Are there ways that Christians might provoke evildoers? If so, when should they modify offensive behavior to avoid conflict, and when must they stand firm to "obey God rather than men"? (Acts 5:29)

8

FORGIVENESS
BILL BAGENTS

There are no perfect people. Romans 3:23 stands just as true today as it did 2,000 years ago. It has been true for every person who has ever lived, with the exception of Jesus Christ (Hebrews 4:15).

It's bad enough that we all sin. But it seems even worse that we all sin against even those whom we love most. In light of this truth, the giving and seeking of forgiveness is a key means by which we can ease life's hurts.

Scripture is filled with outstanding examples of interpersonal forgiveness. Esau forgave Jacob (Genesis 33). Joseph forgave his brothers (Genesis 45 and 50). The prodigal son's father freely forgave him (Luke 15:11–32). Jesus asked the Father to extend mercy to those who were murdering Him (Luke 23:34). As he was being martyred, Stephen beautifully imitated the Lord's example (Acts 7:60).

Scripture not only shows us forgiveness, it commands us to be forgiving. In the model prayer, Jesus taught us to pray: "And forgive us our debts, as we forgive our debtors" (Matthew 6:12). Lest we miss the point, the Lord emphasized it twice more in verses 13 and 14. He linked God's forgiveness toward us to our forgiveness of one another.

Ephesians 4:32 reads, "And be kind to one another, tenderhearted, forgiving one another, just as God in Christ also forgave you." As we forgive, we show that we are truly "followers of God" (Ephesians 5:1). Forgiveness is a sweet word and an even sweeter practice.

BLESSINGS OF FORGIVENESS

The many benefits of practicing forgiveness are well documented in Scripture. We offer the following as a partial list:

- We forgive in order to obey God (Ephesians 4:32, Colossians 3:13).
- We forgive in order to be forgiven by God (Matthew 6:14–15).
- We forgive in order to imitate Christ (Luke 23:34).
- We forgive in order to imitate the Father (Ephesians 4:32 and 5:1).
- We forgive in order to encourage repentance and to "overcome evil with good" (Romans 12:19–21).

- We forgive in order to avoid becoming trapped by bitterness (Ephesians 4:32).
- We forgive in order to maintain the forgiveness which God has extended to us (Matthew 18:21–35).

Given these many benefits, we might well wonder why more people don't practice this virtue. The truth is that, like all good things, forgiveness costs as well as pays.

COSTS OF FORGIVENESS

To forgive, we must honestly face the pain of the wrong which we have suffered. There can be no denial, no repression, and no excuse-making. We dare not attempt to deny the truth or to protect the guilty. At the same time, we dare not deny our hurt, our anger, or the fact that we may be tempted to "hurt them back."

To forgive, we must honestly admit any role that we played in either creating or worsening the offense. This is certainly not an attempt to "blame the victim." Rather, it is an attempt to face the fact that those who wrong us sometimes have our help in doing so. Perhaps it was our bragging which invited their insult. Perhaps it was our selfishness which encouraged them to ignore our needs.

To forgive, we must defy conventional wisdom. We must reject the inferior way of "an eye for an eye and a tooth for a tooth." We must reject the savage concept of "hurt them worse than they hurt you." To forgive, we must be willing to trust God and leave vengeance to Him.

To forgive, we may have to break old habits and patterns. Forgiveness is not always a natural choice. To "love your enemies, bless those who curse you, do good to those who hate you, and pray for those who spitefully use you and persecute you ..." is not the way of this world (Matthew 5:44). Such love is characteristic of the sons of God.

To forgive, we may have to act much better than we feel. It's natural to strike back when others hurt us. Some would say that it's instinctual. We know better. We know that we are made in the image of God (Genesis 1:26–27). But we also know that our emotions are powerful. We must use our minds and our faith to keep them in check. God's word, not our feelings, is our guide.

To forgive, we may even have to empathize with the person who has hurt us. Again, this is not a natural choice. When people hurt us, especially if they hurt us deeply, we tend to vilify and dehumanize them. We think of them as monsters, not men. To practice forgiveness consistently, we must overcome this temptation. We must remember that God loved us and reached out to us through Jesus, even when we were His enemies (Romans 5:6–11). We must see through our pain in order to remember that souls are at stake.

OBSTACLES TO FORGIVENESS

The kind of forgiveness commanded by God often seems at odds with our notion of fairness. It is as if we're letting the offender off "too easy." After all, shouldn't there be consequences for sin? Of course, there should be, and there are. But God sees to the consequences. He frees us from the task of avenging ourselves (Deuteronomy 32:35, Romans 12:19). He leaves us free to forgive.

"But what about the person who doesn't deserve to be forgiven?" This is another aspect of the issue of fairness. In truth, it is a question which seems more pressing than it really is. Who can ever deserve God's forgiveness? Is it the one who has suffered enough? The one who has apologized sufficiently? The one who has made full restitution? When we ask these questions about deserving God's forgiveness, the answer is obvious. No one can ever deserve God's forgiveness, but He offers it anyway. All He asks is that we trust Him and comply with His commandments.

Sadly, when we pose questions of "deserving forgiveness" regarding someone who has wronged us, we often don't see the truth as clearly. We find it difficult even to approximate the grace which God extends to us. We don't want to "play the fool" and be hurt again. We don't want to tempt the person who has wronged us to think that he did no real harm.

As Christians, we do want to encourage responsibility and repentance (Matthew 18:15–17). At the same time, we must carefully monitor our expectations. A part of us may want to see the person who has harmed us suffer for his sin. A part of us may want to exact our pound of flesh. A part of us may want a public display of contrition to prove the sincerity of the offender's repentance. That part of us may well be wanting too much. To imitate Christ, we must overcome these expectations. Scripture clearly urges Christians to treat others better than they deserve (Matthew 5:38-48 & 7:12).

A related obstacle to forgiveness has its roots in Luke 17:3-4. The key sentence reads, "If your brother sins against you, rebuke him; and if he repents, forgive him." Some have understood this sentence to teach that God-approved forgiveness can be offered only after the offending person repents. We must respectfully disagree for the following reasons:

- The point of this passage is to encourage forgiveness rather than to limit the conditions under which it can be offered.
- Demanding that repentance precede our willingness to forgive runs counter to the prayers of Jesus and Stephen (Luke 23:34; Acts 7:60).
- God Himself reached out to us with the offer of forgiveness while we were still His enemies (Romans 5:6-11).
- It is unwise to base our willingness to forgive on the action or inaction of another person.

Luke 17:3-4, like Matthew 18:15, insists that we take a proactive stance when a brother has wronged us. Rather than waiting for him to come to us, we reach out to him. Ideally, we will meet him on the road as he is coming to make things right with us!

Luke 17:3–4 insists that we neither deny nor excuse the wrong that has been done. We are to rebuke our brother—to show him his fault, lovingly and directly—for the sake of his soul and ours (Galatians 6:1–2). If he repents, we are to forgive him freely and to keep no count of the wrong (Matthew 18:22).

We may ask, "But what if he doesn't repent?" If he does not repent, we must resist the temptation to let anger lead to bitterness and evil-speaking (Ephesians 4:26–32). We must resist the temptation to feel that we have failed. The Lord requires that we keep His commandments and follow His example. When we have done so, we have shown a forgiving spirit. We have extended the offer of forgiveness. We cannot rightly hold ourselves responsible if that offer is rejected. There should be no sense of failure in such a case. Obeying God is meant to ease, not compound, life's hurts.

Biblical forgiveness is hard work. It requires honesty, faith, and love. It involves taking emotional risks with a person who has already harmed us. It demands that we examine our own actions and motives. It forbids us the error of assigning vile motives to the person who has harmed us, as if we could see into his heart (1 Samuel 16:7). It insists that we seek to win our brother, the very one who has sinned against us (Matthew 18:15–17).

FORGIVENESS MYTHS

Many seem to believe that we cannot forgive others until they have asked us to. Confession is good for the soul. It is good, right, and helpful to ask forgiveness of those whom we have wronged. At the same time, we must be very careful about withholding the offer of forgiveness until we have been asked.

There are many ways to request forgiveness. I once knew a little boy who, like most little fellows, sometimes broke family rules. On occasion, his misconduct led to a spanking. He had a special way of "making up" with his dad after those episodes. He would come to the den and simply stand by his dad's recliner. It was his way of saying, "I know I did wrong. I don't want things to stay wrong." When his dad set him in his lap and put his arms around him, all was forgiven. Words weren't needed.

"To forgive is to forget" is probably the most common forgiveness myth. We take great comfort in the fact that this is true of God's forgiveness of our sins. Jeremiah 31:34 ends with these words: "For I will forgive their iniquity, and their sin I will remember no more." Hebrews 8:12 quotes this passage, applying it to the new covenant.

God does forgive and forget. But we are not God. Pain tends to imprint in our brains vividly. Forgiveness, as powerful as it is, does not erase our memory of the wrong we have suffered. In my judgment, that fact is a blessing of God. Remembering helps us to be properly watchful, to do what we can to prevent repetition of the same offense. Remembering helps us to be properly grateful. We need to keep thanking God for giving us the power to forgive.

"Forgive and forget" is a dangerous myth. It often leaves good people feeling like they have failed at forgiveness because their memory of the pain remains. Often their frustration keeps growing because the harder they try to forget, the more they seem to remember. This feeling of failure must be rejected. It is a false guilt. A third powerful myth is that forgiveness means welcoming the person who has hurt us back to full and immediate trust. Reconciliation is certainly one key goal of forgiveness. Love forgives. But love does not demand that we trust those who are untrustworthy. Love may well extend a measure of trust, even to one who has done great wrong. Still, that measure of trust may need time to grow. The rule is: the deeper the hurt, the more time will be needed.

Some see this as conditional forgiveness. That is, "I forgive you if your exemplary behavior shows me that you have truly repented." I believe that Scripture teaches us to forgive fully and freely. At the same time, there is a sense in which trust has to be earned. Giving a person the opportunity to prove himself and regain our trust isn't conditional forgiveness. It's what we might call responsible forgiveness.

A fourth forgiveness myth is that forgiveness is a one-time decision and act. The conscious decision to forgive may be made once and for all. More often, especially in cases of deep harm, even that decision is made as part of the process of forgiveness. The decision may be one-time, but the carrying out of that decision may well be an ongoing process.

Forgiveness is complex. Negative feelings can reemerge long after we thought they were through. The person whom we are struggling to forgive may act in ways that make us question our commitment. Satan is likely to tempt us to rescind our decision. But we know that God is faithful. He will stand with us and enable us if we will keep trying to do right (Philippians 2:12–13).

A fifth myth is that forgiving those who have harmed us will always make us feel better. In the long run, this is no myth at all. It always pays to listen to God. In the short run, however, working to forgive may make us feel worse. Friends, especially those who are not Christians, may chide us for letting the person who has harmed us "off the hook." Our own emotions may challenge our decision to forgive. We often face internal tension when we choose to act better than we feel.

How can we counter this myth? We can remind ourselves that we are more than just our feelings. Emotions matter, but truth matters more. The best way to feel better is to do the good that we know to do and to trust God's law of sowing and reaping (Galatians 6:7–10).

The final myth in this lesson is devious. It attacks us at the level of faith. It says, "My forgiveness means that God cannot hold the wrongdoer accountable for his sin." It's not that we want the offender to suffer. It's just that we don't want to stand in the way of God's justice, especially if the offender's repentance proves false.

Perhaps this myth flows from our earthly legal

system. If no one presses charges, then even the guilty go free. We need not be alarmed. We can and should forgive those who trespass against us. This point must be clear: we forgive people, but only God has the power to forgive sins.

We are incapable of any action which could cause God to do wrong. The Lord cannot even be tempted to do wrong (James 1:13). The judge of heaven and earth always does right. That fact alone encourages us to practice forgiveness eagerly and to leave judgment to Him. That is part of God's formula for easing life's hurts.

QUESTIONS FOR DISCUSSION

1. Is practicing forgiveness really as difficult as this lesson seems to imply?
2. In your judgment, what is the most difficult aspect of practicing forgiveness?
3. Why is it important that each of us become skilled in the practice of forgiveness?
4. Which of the blessings of forgiveness do you consider the most important? Why?
5. Which of the obstacles to forgiveness mentioned above do you consider most challenging? Why?
6. Why should we extend the offer of forgiveness to those who have harmed us?
7. Which of the "forgiveness myths" mentioned above do you consider most dangerous? Give reasons for your choice.

9

MARTIAL ARTS AND MARITAL HURTS

JACK P. WILHELM

Without telling anyone, a rather small woman signed up to take a course in martial arts. She wanted to learn techniques of self-defense that she could use against an abusive husband. She thought that with a surprise attack, she could use martial arts to ease the marital hurts she was enduring from him. I did not hear how she came out—or how he did either!

Sometimes, however, spousal abuse is meted out by the wife on the husband. I thought of the case of a rather big man who found himself before a judge in such a case. The judge said to him, "You're 6' 4" tall and weigh well over 200 pounds while she doesn't even weigh 100 pounds. It is a bit illogical that you have all the bruises. How do you explain that?"

The man said, "Well, Judge, it's like this. Due to our sizes, she can't hurt me none and she does seem to get a great deal of pleasure out of it, so I humor her."

FROM THE BEGINNING

The marriage relationship was never planned by God to involve hurts. When God finished "phase one" of his creation, "everything that he had made was good" (Genesis 1:31). However, there was one thing he was not happy with. That was Adam as a bachelor. He said, "It is not good for man to be alone" (Genesis 2:18). So, he made Eve as a helper suitable to him, and the human family began with the marriage relationship which God declared as "honorable in all" (Hebrews 13:4).

So, since marriage was God's idea and was planned by God to maximize the pleasure and companionship of the human family, everyone from that time has "lived happily ever after," right? Hardly. Even that first family experienced keenly felt hurts: They sinned. They lost their free lease on the most favorable living conditions anyone has ever known (Genesis 3:22–24). Adam's job description changed drastically with the addition of a lot of new back breaking work (Genesis 3:17–19). Eve's lot in life and her relationship to Adam was changed (Genesis 3:16), and consequences still trickle down to all females to this day (1 Timothy 2:12–15). Their oldest son killed his younger brother and was severely punished, (Genesis 4:1–16). To have had such a glorious beginning, the hurts that came to the first family must have been keenly felt.

As you read these thoughts today, you must be keenly aware that a lot of changes have occurred in family life since God launched the marriage concept. Many have come during your lifetime. Changes have occurred in the way a family makes its living. From a primarily agrarian society when the entire family worked on the farm and did their work and chores together, now both parents work out of the home in a pressured high-tech society. The family has also changed where it lives, from rural settings to crowded conditions in large cities. The mobility of a family is shown by the fact that as many as one-third of the addresses of mail order concerns are changed each year. Young people have much more mobility and freedom to date without chaperones than their parents had. Today's young ladies do not know what "mad money" is—and probably would feel little inclination to use it on a date! [Ask your grandmother what this is if you are not familiar with the term "mad money."] Intimacy in college dorms was once regulated by a requirement that a door had to be open the "width of a book" when a young lady was visiting a male briefly in his apartment. Ingenuously, many of them hit on the idea of using a book of matches to circumvent the rule!

The role of religion has changed. Family worship as depicted by Robert Burns in "The Cotter's Saturday Night" has given way to a time when families are not even together in worship services, much less in-home devotionals! Vacationing and "week-ending" have also played havoc to consistency in church attendance for many families.

Quite noticeable is a change in moral views and morality. Divorce is often a casual decision, flippantly made, in spite of the fact that "from the beginning it was not so" (Matthew 19:3–9). [A fairly comprehensive summary of divorce is in my book, *Contemporary Concerns of Christians*, p. 161–177.]

Expressions are changed or have taken on new meaning:

- "Till death do us part" and "As long as we both shall live" are now read as "As long as we both shall love."
- "Keeping yourself faithful to him/her only" has become "Until I meet someone else who turns me on."
- "Love, honor, and obey" have become "Love, honor, and negotiate."
- "For better or for worse" has become "As long as I feel you are meeting my needs."
- "What can I do for you?" has become "What can you do for me?"
- "And endow thee with all my worldly goods" has become "Depending on whether there is something in this marriage for me." A man said once, "I didn't want to marry my wife for her money, but I didn't know any other way to get it."

The last time I made a trip with our school choral group, there were 32 students in the chorus. I have wondered how they would have reacted had I told them before leaving on the first day, "We have reason to believe that on this trip we will have a collision and lose 16 of you. We also have reason to believe that even though the other 16 will be able to complete the trip, only 4 of you will say that you had a good time."

Would they have thought more seriously about embarking on it? We may have had wholesale defections! Yet those statistics represent some marriage hurts: Half of the marriages end in divorce and of those who stay married, only 25% evaluate themselves as being happily married. A lot of marital hurt is picked up in their baggage.

Through a mutual friend, I was asked once to perform a wedding for a young lady I did not know. I have not seen her since the ceremony, but I did see the friend about 5 years later. I asked how she was doing. He said, "Since that wedding you did, she has been divorced 3 times and is now planning to marry a 4th time!" With a wry smile, he added, "If there's a bright spot about it at all, it's the fact that she's remarried the same old boy every time!" She had kept recycling him. He said they remarried once and stayed together one night before splitting again. I thought about how much hurt there must have been in all those legal escapades. I'm sure the lawyers who processed the divorces got paid a lot more than those who performed the marriages.

IS THERE ANY EXPLANATION?

When you review God's plan for marriage and know that many good marriages have been thoroughly enjoyed —not just endured or ended—is there any way to identify what has caused so many hurts? There is no way to provide a complete list, but we can suggest some.

EASING LIFE'S HURTS

Some hurts are caused because of the trend to bypass God's plan. The way God planned marriage, it will work to bring happiness if those who enter it will work at it. The most challenging attempt to bypass God's plan today is the "live in" arrangement. Before 1970, it was called "shacking up" and was illegal in every state in the US. About 10% of couples cohabited in 1965, but more than half of today's newlyweds have lived together before marrying. [See an article by Jay Tolson, "No Wedding? No Ring? No Problem" in *U.S. News and World Report*, March 13, 2000, p. 48.] From 1/3 to 1/2 of couples in these arrangements have children, which has a potential for more hurt due to the absence of legal, financial, and custodial rights and responsibilities. The risk for physical and sexual abuse is greater in these arrangements also, according to studies by Popenoe and Whitehead that Tolson cited. In addition to the surface sexual immorality, there is even more cheating on the part of both partners in live-in arrangements.

It is assumed that once a "living-together" couple does marry (which only about 55% of them eventually do). that their compatibility experience will be better. But Tolson adds that, "According to most research, couples who live together—with the possible exception of those who move in already planning to wed—tend to have rockier marriages and a greater risk of divorce ... It could be that people who cohabit are less traditional in their ideas and less reluctant to divorce." The experts are taking the position that cohabitation is not good preparation for marriage! Mona Charen (*TimesDaily*, Florence, AL, March 24, 1999, p. 3B) cited the National

Marriage Project, a private program affiliated with Rutgers University, as saying "the track record of 'living together' is not so great particularly if the goal is a long and happy marriage." She cited a 1992 study that revealed that 46 percent of "prior cohabiters" had a "greater hazard of divorce than non-cohabiters." Those with "serial cohabitations before marriage have much higher divorce rates than those who lived with only one person." Some of the hurts were "heartbreak and instability" and "loneliness," and the relationship "becomes more hollow and more brittle."

One of the greatest hurts the National Marriage Project spotlighted was "that cohabitation is most harmful for children." Charen cited a British study that found that "children living with mom and her boyfriend were 33 times more likely to be abused physically and sexually than the children living with both biological parents."

Some hurts are caused by inadequate preparation and forethought before marriage is entered. Sometimes one or both in a marriage have faulty ideology or improper motivation and marry the wrong person for the wrong reason. Ideally, the preferred reasons for marrying should be love, respect, desire for companionship and posterity, a healthy sexual relationship (1 Corinthians 7:1-5), and a wholesome desire to enjoy the fullness of life that God intended marriage to provide. Peter called it a dimension in which a couple can be "heirs together of the grace of life" (1 Peter 3:7).

There are so many improper motivations for marrying that they all cannot be listed. A few might be these: greed, exploitation, seeking stability for insecurities, pity, accepting a dare, a "mother hen" desire to reform one, distorted "romance" impulses, social expectancy, career advancement, a "cover up" for immorality or a taboo lifestyle, to spite another, and financial desperation.

In a society in which numbers of young people give much more thought to the purchase of their first automobile than they do to the selection of a marriage partner for life, it is urgent that parents and the church give some serious attention to the values we are instilling in our youth. Some hurts are caused because fair expectations and needs are not met in marriage.

A young couple may abruptly end their marriage and go separate ways as casually as buying a new wardrobe. I have heard of some who separated at the reception following their wedding ceremony! I think it was an exaggeration, as was once reported, that one couple split because one got a bigger piece of cake than the other. However, the root cause of many hurts is selfishness and immaturity. Is there a way to know when a couple is mature enough to marry?

WHEN IS ONE READY FOR MARRIAGE?

One is not ready merely because he reaches a certain age chronologically. Is one old enough to marry merely because he/she is old enough to drive, vote, enter the military, legally marry, or even as old as their parents were when they married? Remember that years ago, a boy who married as a teen may already have made two or three crops and managed a farm, or a teenaged girl may have helped raise some siblings and kept house so the rest of the family could work in the fields. Their tasks had disciplined them earlier to accept responsibilities that some today have been spared. I remember a tenth-grade girl in a class who was asked once to go get a mop from the custodian to deal with a spill in class; she said, "What's a mop?"

One is not ready for marriage merely because some milestone has been reached in life. Some seem to think that—especially if they have completed high school, or been discharged from a military stint, or had a job training course, or read a marriage manual, or completed a prison term, or studied a marriage preparation course at church or in school.

One may not be ready merely because he or she says, "I'm in love!" Many mistake infatuation for love. And sometimes they mistake jealousy for love when it could be merely the badge of a loser who knows he can't keep a girl interested in him in any way except by making jealous demands.

One is not ready for marriage merely because he or she is physically mature. Readiness for marriage requires that one be emotionally mature as well as physically mature. A lot of hurts can come to a couple who are not able to think independently and objectively. Maturity means that they are willing to pay the price in advance for desired future rewards. The prisons and the divorce courts are full of hurting people who never learned to sacrifice to meet goals and make marriage work.

Some hurts in marriage are caused by in-law interference. God stressed the "leave and cleave" strategy (Genesis 2:24), and it was reaffirmed by Jesus: "A man shall leave his father and mother and be joined to his wife, and the two shall become one flesh" (Matthew 19:5). The matter was stressed again by Paul after the church began in Ephesians 5:31.

The threat of in-law interference has prompted some glib advice: "A newly married couple ought to live at least 500 miles away from both sets of parents, across three rivers, two of which do not have bridges."

There is a report that "The Pentagon once did a study on why so many American Servicemen marry women in the countries where they're stationed. Contrary to popular belief, loneliness had nothing to do with it. Once the men rotated back to the US, all their in-laws were thousands of miles away."

In my wife's book, *Worthy Women*, you will find a good discussion of in-law relationships. Together, we compiled some suggestions that spotlighted some hot spots where difficulties arise in marriage.

In one study of in-law interference, for example, one half of all complaints about mothers-in-law involved three traits: She (1) meddles, interferes, and is nosey, (2) is possessive, demanding, and over-protective, and (3) nags, criticizes, and ridicules. A frequent criticism of fathers-in-law was that they were uncongenial, intolerant, and old-fashioned. Brother-in-law complaints were that they were incompetent and lazy. A few other areas of complaint were that they are thoughtless, overstay and abuse hospitality, and are too talkative and gushy without listening. Obviously, these are all traits that

Christians should work to eliminate, whether they are in-law problems or not. [See F. Phillip Rice, *Marriage and Parenthood*, Allyn and Bacon: Boston, 1979, p. 403.]

Some of the areas of potential conflict listed in my wife's book that a young couple may expect to come up with in-laws were these:

- Where to spend holidays
- How often to visit in-laws and how long to stay
- How much to spend on gifts and what occasions to remember
- Whether to accept loans or excessive gifts
- Frequency of communication, phone calls, etc.
- How to react to advice offered
- Interference in rearing children
- How to relate to in-laws who are not Christians (or who do not act as Christians should!)
- Employment in family businesses
- Whether you will share housing
- Responsibility assumed for care of aging parents
- How much independence can you insist on without guilt

Perhaps all of these factors are exaggerations, since some parents-in-law have been of tremendous help to struggling young couples without interference. But there are times when interference has been real, and hurts have been deep. It may help for one to remember that he cannot have in-laws without being an in-law. A practice of the Golden Rule and giving others the benefit of the doubt could go a long way in easing hurts of this type. A wise couple will make a mature pact with each other that they will not let any third party come between them as long as each is applying a Christian solution to each difficulty that arises.

Some hurts in marriage are caused by irresponsibility. Both people in the marriage have individual responsibilities. If one or both shirk them, hurts will ensue. Selfishness is at the root of some irresponsibility and incompatibility. The absentee mate is an example of irresponsibility. A woman once wrote to Ann Landers to tell of a husband who would be gone for 5 to 7 years at a time and then show up as if he had merely been out to buy a paper. The biggest puzzle about the case was that he had done that about three times, and she had still allowed him to come back!

The non-supportive mate is usually identified as the one who does not pay alimony and child support. Many states are now becoming more aggressive to make them meet their responsibilities. If one does not provide for his own, he/she is strongly rebuked by 1 Timothy 5:8. However, another factor may need consideration to be fair: Would you feel good about paying child support if you had reason to believe that the funds were not used wisely for the children's needs, if you had no rights to see the children, and if you had reason to believe that the children were given intentionally slanted false impressions about you?

Independent of finances, there is also such a thing as not providing emotional support to the mate while sitting in the same room. Counselors have said the most repeated pain they hear rehearsed by their clients is a husband who feels he gets little respect from his wife and a wife who feels she gets little love from her husband. Dr. Marlin Howe has said, "God designed marriage to have a healthy dependent/co-dependent relationship (Genesis 1–2). The wife is to be dependent upon her husband. He is to be dependent upon her dependency. In doing so, she feels feminine, protected, cared for. He feels masculine, needed, and important. She feels loved. He feels respected (Ephesians. 5)." He adds, "I have never yet met a woman who respected a man she could control. I have never yet met a man who truly loved a woman who controlled him."

A lot of hurt in marriage is caused by infidelity. God considers this problem in marriage so important that he reserves judgment about it to himself: "Marriage is honorable among all, and the bed undefiled; but fornicators and adulterers God will judge" (Hebrews 13:4). Jesus considered it important enough to allow adultery as a justifiable cause for remarriage for one who might be truly innocent in a failed marriage (Matthew 19:3–9).

Even though an affair is a shocking hurt in marriage, it is not impossible for a couple to forgive and recover. Psychologists Tom Wright and Nancy Glass, "currently studying couples recovering from affairs, find that not only do two thirds decide to stay together, but many report newfound richness and closeness gained through conquering the ordeal together." [See "A Lens on Matrimony," *U.S. News and World Report* by Joannie M. Schrof, February 21, 1994, p. 66 ff.]

The Bible story of Hosea and Gomer and the forgiving spirit Jesus expressed to the woman in John 8 have been an encouragement to many who want to recover from this hurt. With reference to those who experience many hurts caused by immoral lifestyles, the teaching of Paul in 1 Corinthians 6:11 has also offered great encouragement: "And such were some of you. But you were washed, but you were sanctified, but you were justified in the name of the Lord Jesus and the Spirit of our God." It reminds of the basic truth of the gospel: No one ever has to stay the way he is!

QUESTIONS FOR DISCUSSION

1. Discuss some of the changes you have observed during your lifetime that you feel are good for marriage and family life.
2. Discuss some changes of recent years that you feel have been harmful to marriage and family life.
3. What has changed in recent years about the role of religion in family life? What do you think the church should do to cope with needs of young people approaching marriage?
4. What do you feel has contributed to the attitude of society to accept "living together" without disapproval?
5. What would you say to a close friend who

confided in you, "I am thinking of getting a divorce because my needs are not being met"? Would your comments be different if the person were not a Christian?
6. How can parents legitimately help their children when they marry without their assistance becoming harmful interference?
7. Have "mothers-in-law" been unfairly stigmatized in an uncomplimentary way?
8. Are there limits to which forgiveness and fresh starts can be offered to family members who are irresponsible and unfaithful?

10

MARITAL STRESS
BILL BAGENTS

Marital stresses are nothing new. I don't say that to imply that such pressures are either minor or unimportant. All pain is uniquely personal. Most of us know that there's not much pain that is worse than family pain.

It may help us to remember that we are not alone when we face marital stress. Every couple faces challenges. Scripture offers us many examples of difficulties within marriage.

- Adam invited trouble when he blamed Eve for his sin (Genesis 3:12).
- Abram and Sarai created trouble when they tried to "help" the Lord fulfill his promise through Hagar (Genesis 16 and 21).
- Isaac and Rebekah insured trouble when they each chose a favorite child (Genesis 25:28).

MARITAL STRESS

- Jacob created major stress by marrying both Leah and Rachel (Genesis 29-30).
- Samson distressed his parents and himself through his choice of a Philistine wife (Judges 14).
- Elkanah could probably tell us why God's plan is for marriage between one man and one woman (1 Samuel 1).
- Solomon's wives turned his heart away from God (1 Kings 11).
- Ahasuerus's pride and drinking created the crisis with Vashti, his queen (Esther 1).
- Had not the angel intervened; Mary's miraculous pregnancy would have ended her betrothal to righteous Joseph (Matthew 1:18–25).

These examples remind us that conflict within marriage is not unexpected. Sometimes, it arises from our own sin. Sometimes, it stems from the sins of others. Sometimes, it even flows from an unexpected blessing. Stress and conflict are not, in and of themselves, sinful. However, sin often accompanies our attempts to handle these pressures.

ONE STEP BACK

Many marital conflicts begin before the marriage itself. One key cause has been described as "running the red lights." "Red lights" or "red flags" are negative, dangerous, and often sinful behaviors which become obvious during the dating process. Key "red lights" include:

- Excessive fussing and arguing. See Ephesians 4:29–32.
- Jealousy, which is often manifested in over-possessiveness or attempts to control the other person.
- Financial instability or irresponsibility.
- The absence of a strong work ethic. See Ephesians 4:28 and Proverbs 24:30–34. Back home, they tell the story of the man who was "a real go-getter." He took his wife to work every morning at 8:00. Then, at 5:00 pm, he'd go get her.
- Use of alcohol or other drugs. See Proverbs 20:1 and 23:29–35.
- Dishonesty. See John 8:44 and Ephesians 4:25.
- Impulsiveness, lack of self-control. See Proverbs 16:32.
- Love of money. See Proverbs 22:1 and 23:4–5, Ecclesiastes 5:10–11, and 1 Timothy 6:3–19.
- Mistreatment of the young or the elderly.
- Religious differences. Those outside Christ are spiritually dead. While that fact grieves us, it should also warn us. A home without God as its head lacks the key source of strength and stability.

As we noted in Chapter Two, "The Limits of Love," many seem to believe that they can change their spouse after marriage. Though possible, such is most unlikely. The far more common rule is that whatever raises concerns during dating gets worse after marriage. It is just plain foolish to marry someone under the illusion that key sources of conflict will just go away.

UNREALISTIC EXPECTATIONS

Many seem to enter marriage with unrealistic expectations. They remember the fairy tales where everyone "lives happily ever after." In their more rational moments, they'll admit that such is hardly likely. Sadly, we're not always rational.

Some marry and expect to begin housekeeping at the same level it took their parents twenty years to achieve. They were too young to remember the early days of their parents' greatest sacrifice and struggle. When parents tell them those stories, they sound like myths that "old folks" have created to discourage the young.

Some marry and expect their spouse to know just what pleases them—from the way they want their socks folded to the brand of bread they buy. It's as if the wedding ceremony was somehow supposed to infuse their mate with all the knowledge that they'd ever need. We know that's not possible. Even if it were, our tastes have a way of changing. Like it or not, each of us is a moving target.

Some marry and expect a perfect relationship. The husband will know and "step up to" his role. The wife will prove to be the perfect complement and companion. Each forgets that the marriage roles learned from their respective parents are the only pattern which they know well. We all tend to think of the way we were reared as normal. No wonder there is so much role confusion!

One of the dearest couples we've ever known had "his money" and "her money," and never the twain did meet. He paid "his bills" and she paid "hers." That is foreign to Laura and me. We'd never dream of trying that approach. But it worked for them. It had been working for them for decades.

Sometimes we hear a husband lament, "I just don't know how to get along with my wife. She's not the same girl I married!" I suspect that's pretty accurate. Within the biblical guidelines of Ephesians 5:22–33, each couple continually defines and redefines their respective roles. For example, to date I've been married to a teenager, a college student, a pregnant lady, a mother of one, a mother of two, a graduate student, and a full-time teacher—and all of them have been the same lady! She's been married to a guy who has his own set of ever-changing issues. Even though our core values have remained grounded in Scripture, our marriage has been an adventure. We should have expected nothing less. Every marriage is!

DEVELOPMENTAL PRESSURES

Developmental pressures refer to the normal, anticipated stresses which we encounter through the life-cycle of our family. Though some families skip some "steps," we find no difficulty in recognizing each of them as unique stages. Sometimes, just knowing that each stage presents its own challenges may help us face them more wisely. The literature varies somewhat in the details, but the following is a basic standard approach.

In the premarital stage, each potential partner is assessing the other. Stress accompanies this evaluative process, especially if serious interest is present. We should note that the common American (Western) version of dating is a recent invention. Historically, far more marriages have been arranged by the families of the couple. The many weaknesses of modern dating have spawned a growing body of literature opposing the process altogether.

After the wedding, the husband and wife form the marital dyad. Each begins to discover just how much was not learned about the other during the dating process. Stresses include where to spend each respective holiday, how to handle the checkbook, and who fills each vital role within the home. Preferably, the couple will spend notable time in this "bonding stage" before moving to the next. Some recommend waiting two to four years before having children.

We all have strong assumptions about the proper roles of husband and wife. Some men see their job as their job. At home, they're "off duty." Even when both partners work outside the home, the lion's share of the "homework" often falls on the wife. Wise men know better. Wise couples know that as much as they love and have learned from their parents, they must now agree on the roles each will fill in their new (and unique) home.

This takes some doing! And, most of that doing involves trial-and-error.

The birth of the first child begins the family triad: baby makes three. Even when planned and anticipated with joy, this is a particularly stressful period. The mother encounters impressive (or should we say, oppressive?) physical demands. Everyone stays tired. Babies are expensive. Going anywhere seems like moving.

Sadly, some conflicted couples believe that having a baby is the answer to their problems. "It'll make us grow up" and "It'll give us more reason to stay together" are two common statements. For troubled marriages, such statements just aren't true. Having a child is adding pressure to an already difficult situation.

It begins during the triad stage and continues through the completed family years. Husband and wife are now dad and mom as well. What parenting style will they follow? How will corrective discipline be practiced? How will limited resources be allocated to best serve the family? When handled well, these issues strengthen the marriage. When handled poorly, the endless debates lead to fragmentation.

Even if parenting issues are effectively managed, every child grows into a teenager. The family with teens is unique. Mark Twain is credited with the following quote, "When the child turns thirteen, put him in a barrel and feed him through the knothole. When he turns sixteen, plug the hole." He wasn't the first to notice that the teen years are often difficult.

As children become teens, their parents often have entered middle age. The teenagers are approaching physical maturity, while their parents may well be experiencing the first undeniable signs of physical decline. As teens test the limits of their maturity and independence, conflict may escalate—both in frequency and intensity.

Couples who practice parenting as a team will find themselves communicating with one another on an ever-higher level. The needs of the family force them to. Those who have not developed a teamwork approach will find the increasing pressure of parenting teens putting even more stress on their marriage. The marriage and family literature suggests that this strain, along with the legendary midlife crisis which often comes during this stage of family life, are major contributors to divorce.

"Launching" is one name for the stage which follows. High school is completed, and the college years begin. Couples with strong marriages often experience this period as a major positive. With the lessened demands of parenting, they have more time and energy to invest in the marriage.

For couples with conflicted marriages, all major changes in the family system tend to expose the weaknesses in their relationship. This is especially true for "helicopter parents." Helicopter parents are those whose lives revolve around their children, to the neglect of their marriage. As they "launch" their children, they also launch their key reason for being together. Marital stress is sure to increase.

I grew up hearing the modern proverb, "The best thing that a father can do for his children is to love their mother." By God's design, the marital relationship forms the core of family strength. Whatever strengthens a marriage blesses the entire family. Whatever weakens a marriage is a grave danger.

The post-launching period can be a time of tremendous blessing. The children are now "on their own." The joys of grand parenting begin. Retirement may allow travel. It certainly allows more discretion in the allocation of time. But all these blessings presume an on-going healthy, loving relationship. Such relationships don't just happen. They are gifts from God which are maintained and enhanced as marriage partners continue to grow in love and devotion.

Again, change is not the friend of a conflicted marriage. Even a much-anticipated retirement may not be a blessing for every marriage. Perhaps you have heard about the couple who got along quite well until they both retired. Their explanation for the post-retirement conflict was simple, "When we were still working, we didn't see one another enough to fight. Even when we did, we were both just too tired."

Development is change. Some have even said that life is change. This could be quite depressing were it not for our faith in God. He is the changeless one (James 1:17). His word is the changeless truth. It both changes and equips us (John 17:17; 2 Timothy 3:14–17). Faithfully following the teaching of Scripture is the key to preventing and overcoming marital stress (Proverbs 31; Ephesians 5:22–33; Titus 2:1–8).

A MODERN ASSAULT ON TRUTH AND MARRIAGE

Sadly, many now view biblical teaching on marriage as hopelessly old-fashioned. Some even attack the biblical model as abusive and hopelessly unfair. This is particularly true in the case of Ephesians 5:22–24, which reads,

> Wives, submit to your own husbands as to the Lord. For the husband is the head of the wife, as also Christ is head of the church; and He is the Savior of the body. Therefore, just as the church is subject to Christ, so let wives be to their own husbands in everything.

Some view this paragraph as encouraging male domination within marriage. Others see it as creating a climate of abuse and oppression. We need to know and to teach that Ephesians 5 is not about domination, abuse, or oppression. The biblical concept of submission is not something that one demands of another or "lords over" another. Rather, it is humility in action. It is an attitude which Christians willingly choose on a number of levels.

- We submit to the laws of our government (Romans 13:1–7; Titus 3:1–2).
- We submit to our "masters" (1 Peter 2:18–25). This principle applies to bosses or anyone in authority over us today.

- Wives submit to their husbands (Ephesians 5:22–24; 1 Peter 3:1–6).
- Younger people submit to their elders, particularly to their parents (Ephesians 6:1–4; Colossians 3:20–21).
- All Christians are to be submissive toward one another, especially to our spiritual leaders (Ephesians 5:21; 1 Peter 5:5; Hebrews 13:17)
- Biblically speaking, submission is never forced on a wife by her husband. Wives respect their husbands as part of their loyalty to Christ. Husbands love and respect their wives as part of their faith as well (Ephesians 5:33). Husbands lead the home, but they do so as servant leaders. They lead in love, following the example of Christ (Ephesians 5:25–30). They follow the biblical mandate, "Likewise you husbands, dwell with them [your wives] with understanding, giving honor to the wife …" (1 Peter 3:7).

Love, honor, respect, and faith form the basis for biblical submission. Such submission is powerful. It demonstrates our reliance on God. It follows the example of Christ. It helps create marriages in which joy and peace abound. Where love is maximized, marital stress is minimized. This, too, is a blessing of God.

QUESTIONS FOR DISCUSSION

1. Why do you think the Bible offers so many examples of difficulties within marriage?
2. What "red lights" (negative behaviors that should slow or stop the dating process) would you add to the list offered in this lesson?
3. Does every marriage involve some degree of unrealistic expectations? Explain.
4. In your opinion, which of the developmental pressures discussed above is the most dangerous? Why?
5. Has this lesson over-emphasized the pressures that the normal changes of life can put on a marriage? Explain.
6. In what ways has the Bible's teaching on submission within marriage been abused?
7. Is submission within marriage an outdated concept? Give reasons for your answer.

11

CHILD REARING HURTS

JACK P. WILHELM

I remember once that Ann Landers asked her readers who were parents to inform her as to whether they would choose to have children again if it was a choice they could make. Over 70% of those who responded said that they would not. Of course, it is possible that those who were not "satisfied customers" might have had a higher motivation to reply.

I thought of the lady who was asked that same question, whether she would have children again if given the choice. She said, "Yes, but not the same ones!"

God did not intend for children to be unhappy experiences—for them or for their parents. The Psalmist declared that children "are a heritage from the Lord. The fruit of the womb is his reward. Like arrows in the hand of a warrior, so are the children of one's youth. Happy is the man who has his quiver full of them," (Psalm 127:3–5).

In spite of the happiness children can bring to

parents, a number of young couples are apprehensive about having children. Potential grandparents are sometimes torn, desiring grandchildren yet fearful of what might lie ahead if they had them. They have seen heartbreaking scenes of good parents who are victimized by their own offspring. The tales of terror are not all fictitious flicks on the screen or the tube. They have seen malicious young rebels without a cause turn into demanding ingrates, brimming with churlish, insolent fury toward authority figures.

The defiant ones snarl at parents and society with bared teeth and doubled fists. With some of them, no amount of love seems adequate to break the caldron of contempt welled up inside.

At times, the story shifts to the heart-rending shock of youth who end their own lives senselessly or go on violent rampages like the school shootings. Parents are not the only ones unable to reach them. Teachers, guidance counselors, and social workers alike are viewed as part of the adult world that they feel betrayed them, and they want no part of the belated concern, however sincerely it may be offered. The horrendous school shootings that have shocked us have left hurts and scars that will never heal in countless innocent victims.

Is there any help? There are pitfalls in some children that no parents can circumvent, such as mental illness, emotional instability, and a self-willed temperament that resists training. Even the most gifted, trained professionals are still trying to unlock the secrets of those issues. Hurts still occur in spite of best efforts.

But assuming that a child is free of serious block

buster traits and has normal drives and learning ability, what then? A pattern of success has been observed. The children of conscientious Christian parents who are introduced early to God and healthy spiritual values in a loving way have the edge. They are led to feel empathy and sympathy for others. They are disciplined firmly but lovingly and consistently. They feel secure if they have the personal bodily presence of both parents, but they know also that their parents are concerned and informed about what they are doing when they are apart.

That combination—parental presence and parental firmness with love—goes together. The absence of both of those factors is usually catastrophic, and the absence of either one of them is less effective than the other by itself. Unfortunate circumstances sometimes dictate that a single parent has to shoulder the entire burden. Even then, the above recipe administered unilaterally is still their best shot. A parent who is present but indulgent, or a parent who is firm but absent or inconsistent does not have the edge and parents who are both absent and indulgent do not have a prayer in a modern, fast-paced society where children slip away from us so quickly.

This may mean at times that parents have to be firmer than they prefer in dealing with their children. Edsel Burleson used to tell the story of a tall, graceful American girl who won the Wimbledon tennis tournament and was crowned by Queen Elizabeth II. The girl's life had always been one struggle after another. When she was very young, she was exceedingly ill, and her convalescence was remarkably slow.

Her mother discovered that the girl just wanted to

sit and be inactive. Her mother told her to bring a slab of rock from the barn to the house to serve as a footstep. The girl was shocked; she told her mother there was no way she could move it. Her mother said, "Move it! I don't care if you only move it one inch a day, move it!"

It took the girl two months, but she moved it. And she learned a great lesson: Although she was weak, she grew to be strong by struggle. Her name was Althea Gibson. That rock may have been a more fitting symbol than a crown to signify what designated her as a champion.

THE NEED FOR STRESSING TIME TESTED VALUES

The practicality of stressing the time worn values has been given validity in a number of research projects. Frank Goble, in an article entitled "Can Your Children Succeed Without Your Help?" (in *Success Unlimited*, July 1973) quoted the results of a research project in which Dr. Richard H. Blum studied 1,000 middle class parents and their children over a 3-year period. The results?

The researchers concluded that children of permissive parents had a far greater chance to become hooked on hard drugs than those whose parents were strict but affectionate. "As scientists," writes Blum, "we were surprised to find that the best protection a child can have against drugs is the old-fashioned group of moral values. Families that believed in God and in Country, went to church regularly, loved their children but disciplined them strictly and respected the police were not bothered with a drug problem. But families that believed children must be free to "find themselves," that practice no religion or very little and that mistrusted or were disrespectful to authority generally had youngsters who took drugs."

Perhaps there is a clue in these findings as to why many parents are experiencing "hurts" when children disappoint them—namely that people are surprised that the old-fashioned moral values work! I realize that this study was conducted some time ago, but in over 50 years of observing more than two generations of young people, I will say unreservedly that the conclusions of the study were valid then and the strategy will still work today. I realize that "times have changed" and the pressures for today's children to be involved in the drug scene and immorality that is encouraged by a relaxed cultural climate are great. I realize that we may need to use more relevant approaches and communication styles, but the basic principles outlined in that study are still valid.

Charles Eliot, a former president of Harvard, once said, "Nobody knows how to teach morality effectively without religion." Our nation is now paying a heavy price for having made education a god and removing God from education. The late Judge Sam Davis Tatum who served over 40 years as a juvenile court judge in Nashville once stated that of all of the thousands of young people who were brought before him with problems, there were only a few times when the children were regular attendants in church activities when the incident occurred that brought them into court—and even fewer appeared before him whose parents attended services regularly also.

Al and Linda Behel have served as family counselors for many years in Knoxville. They have stressed some things that every child needs in parents, some of which are:

- Stability. A shaky parent causes a disintegrated ego in the child. He needs to see someone he can trust to be the same tomorrow and the next day and the next.
- Love. Love must be consistent and communicated to the child unconditionally.
- A Consistent Value System. The parent is the primary role model of values for children. Inconsistency leads to disintegration and disorientation for the child.
- An Example, A Model of Behavior. If you will check, throughout the Old Testament, problem children had problem parents whose examples were lacking.
- The Ability to Share Problems and Joys. Parents must listen to the little things (e.g. childish pleasures and childhood "sweethearts" etc.) before the youngster will feel free to discuss the "big" ones.
- A Parent Who Grows with Him/Her. Children differ at each level of development, and parents must allow for these differences.

Allow the child to grow up. Don't keep him/her dependent on you.

Al added some thoughts that are helpful in childrearing:

- Parents have more power than they will ever need—if used properly.
- When you're out of control, the child is in control.
- Use action to get action, not emotion to get action.
- Use misbehavior as an opportunity for the child to grow-not as an opportunity for you to vent your anger.
- Remember: There are battles you can win and battles you cannot win. Never fight one you cannot win. Don't make rules you cannot enforce.

GETTING THE RIGHT START

I hear a lot of grandparents today say, "I would be scared to be starting out as a new parent today. The values in today's world are so diluted, and the pressures on young parents are so keen, I am not sure we could succeed."

That also prompts another observation that I have heard often: "God knew what he was doing when he arranged for the young to have children." There is a sense of courage and invincibility about being young that makes them numb to fear. It may well be that every

CHILD REARING HURTS

generation of new parents had some of the same pressures.

My wife and I were fortunate in the early years of our parenting experiences to have two good pediatricians, Dr. Sam Carney in Madison, Tennessee, and Dr. Jim Middleton in Florence, Alabama. Their medical knowledge, their concern, and their practical communication skills were very helpful. When we first met Dr. Carney, our first son was about a year old. Dr. Carney said, "There are two kinds of mothers I like to help take care of their babies. One is the young teenage mother who is living about 2,000 miles away from her mother. When the grandmother is not around daily to overrule everything, the new mother is totally helpless and will do what I say. The other one is the mother who has already had 7 or 8 children and then has another one. By then she'll listen to anybody!"

As we got into the "terrible twos" and wondered what was next, Dr. Carney said, "There's only one thing you can say for sure about a 2-year old, and that is that in another year, he'll be 3 if nothing happens to him." Dr. Middleton picked up a few years later with his expertise when we moved back to Florence. I have always appreciated the fact that he called our home one morning about 8 a.m. to ask how David was doing. We had not contacted him, but Dr. Middleton had dreamed about two a.m. that we had called to tell him David was sick and to ask for advice. The dream was so real that he wanted to call back and check on him. Most people can't get a doctor to return a call when a child is sick, but when you have a doctor who will call you when you don't even need him yet, young insecure parents have a lot to be thankful for!

But time passed, and, as one lady said, "We had bad luck with our children. They all grew up and began homes of their own." Nearly all mothers at one time or another have wished they could have those little ones still crying, and spilling, and fussing, and laughing throughout the house. They have admitted that the greatest joys of their lives were the times when their little ones were still under foot.

BUT WHAT ABOUT CHILDREN WHO DISAPPOINT?

One of my former students once spent a summer selling Bibles in Florida. To demonstrate the features of his Bible, he would show prospective customers how to use its concordance and find familiar verses. When the summer was over, he said the one verse that more people wanted him to find than any other was Proverbs 22:6. He said, "Parents, with tears in their eyes, would say 'Where's that verse that says if you train up a child right, he will always be faithful?' Then they might add, 'We tried to bring ours up right, but they have caused us a lot of hurt. We want to know where we went wrong'."

The verse they were referring to says, "Train up a child in the way he should go, and when he is old, he will not depart from it" (Proverbs 22:6).

When people read this verse, the usual immediate assumption is that parents have the exclusive, inescapable duty to train their children and if one of them ever goes astray, it is proof positive that the parent failed. But if that conclusion is always true, what about the following?

Wouldn't all children have to be alike? Are they? If you think so, just try having another one!

Wouldn't all parents have to be alike and use identical methods? But very seldom would any two parents be identical in their philosophies and approaches, much less all other sets of parents.

Would it also not have to be true that no other influences except the parents would affect the child in any way? But other influences are there. And other scriptures are true, like 1 Corinthians 15:33 that teaches that "Evil company corrupts good habits."

If there are significant variables in children, parents, grandparents, peers, and methods, then would there not have to be a divine overriding of all variables to guarantee uniform results? Yet we know that the day of modern miracles ended, as in 1 Corinthians 13:8ff.

Further, if we assume that a child is properly trained, then would we have to accept "the impossibility of apostasy" so that he could not fall or depart from the truth when he became an adult? If so, that assumption would violate all the warnings given about apostasy.

These dilemma have caused some to assume something else about Proverbs 22:6. They doubt that the passage is true! Surely there must be some other factors involved.

QUESTIONS THAT HAVE A BEARING ON PROVERBS 22:6

What does the word train mean? Guy N. Woods said, "The word 'train' means vastly more than to impart instruction. It translates the Hebrew verb *chanak*, the primary meaning of which is 'to put in one's mouth,' and figuratively, to initiate, to lay the groundwork of character, to instill principle," (Guy N. Woods, *Questions and Answers*, Open Forum, p. 192.)

The word seems to refer to all of the influences that contribute to the development of a child. It can involve telling, teaching, example, guidance, counseling, discipline and correction (or lack of it), restraint, advice, associations, and the influences and impressions absorbed from all directions.

Who does the training? Parents will be involved of course, since they get the children first and usually are around them most in those early formative years. But notice that the parents are not directly mentioned in Proverbs 22:6. (Fathers are not mentioned until v. 28, and in a different context then.)

Many other influences are a part of the training process (the "putting in the mouth" and "imparting groundwork for character") of the children. Grandparents have a part—and unfortunately at times they try to undo or thwart what the parents try to do! Teachers and ministers and other church folks may be as influential as the parents, especially as the children get older. That is how cults succeed! And in some cases, they are around the children more than parents are once the children begin school.

Peers and companions are sometimes rated as the number one influence on children. Neighbors and casual acquaintances have their part, in the spirit of Tennyson's line, "I am a part of all that I have met." And then there is the matter of all that children read, see, hear, and absorb from all sources including the Internet, MTV, and the rest of the media! It is easy enough for those who have no children to say, "Good parents must control all of these things!"

It is said that the Great Wall of China was built as security against invading forces. It was supposed to protect because it was too high to climb over and too wide to turn over. Yet in its first 100 years, China was invaded three times when the enemy bribed the gate keepers and marched through. The best parents can try, but the influences are still going to break through in spite of best efforts. There are limits to what even "good parents" can do regarding isolation and control of children without violating Ephesians 6:4 and Colossians 3:21 which do not permit abuse. Ideally, we hope and pray that the child can develop self-control rather than depend only on external controls.

What bearing do heredity and environment have in the training process? Environment apparently is important, as suggested in the warning in 1 Corinthians 15:33 and other passages that tell us to "avoid the appearance of evil." However, it must not be the total factor because Samuel was reared in the same environment as the sons of Eli. Samuel turned out well, but Eli's sons did not.

Both Eli and Samuel had problem children. Eli was rebuked because "he restrained them not," (1 Samuel 3:13), but Samuel was not rebuked as Eli was. Also, the cases of Joseph and Daniel show that one can be good even in a bad environment. Parental effort and environment may vary; the duty of the child to do right remains.

Heredity and "individual differences" seem to be a factor also. Remember that Proverbs 22:6 said the child should be trained "in the way that he should go." That means, "according to the tenor of his way" as the Hebrew phrase suggested, that is, in harmony with his disposition, natural talents, and individual character. (See Woods also on this in *Questions and Answers*, p. 192.)

All of this seems to be another way of saying that we are not all alike. There are natural differences and varying temperaments. Paul recognized this when he said in Romans 12:18, "If it is possible, as much as depends on you, live peaceably with all men." [The KJV says, "As much as in you is ... "] Some children, from birth, are simply more compliant and have an easy-going temperament. They require very little restraint. Others are strong willed, rebellious, and resistant to correction and control. We all know some godly families who succeeded with a number of children but may still have had one who was not of the same "temperament" or "tenor" as the others.

Does a child have any responsibility in his own training process? Regarding Eli's sons, we might notice that "his sons made themselves vile ..." (1 Samuel 3:13). A child who knows right from wrong has an increased personal duty to do right, regardless of parental permissiveness. The process of training is not a one-way street, involving only the parents. It is not complete until the child accepts the training.

We seem not to have as much trouble understanding this concept in other areas. I may give to you an object, but the process of my giving it to you is not complete until you take it from my hand. I give; you take. A teacher teaches; the pupil learns. The process of learning (training) is not complete until something happens inside the student. God gives us salvation by his grace; we will never be saved until we accept it.

So in the training process, the parent provides the teaching, the telling, the example, the guided oversight, the correction, the love, the discipline, the exhortation to "put in one's mouth" or "instill principle and character" in the child, but he is still not "trained in the way he should go" until his response is positive in accepting the process.

Remember, Eli's sons were punished for their behavior. Why, if the fault was all Eli's? Solomon, the very person God used to give us Proverbs 22:6, was offered training by his father, David, in 1 Chronicles 28:9ff. And Solomon was also taught directly by God! (2 Chronicles 7:17ff) Yet he turned to other gods! Are we going to say, "God, you must not have been a good teacher! Your son, Solomon, turned out bad!" Solomon turned to other gods "when he was old" because other influences overpowered his earlier exposure to what he was taught. His foreign wives turned him away from God (1 Kings 11:1–13).

CONCLUSION

This lesson is not intended in any way to excuse negligent parents who make no effort to provide wholesome training to their children. But it may well suggest that it is time for godly parents who really tried to train their children to the best of their ability to stop beating themselves over the head and wringing their hands in despair and guilt because of children who bring them hurt by being wayward.

Every one of us must give an account of ourselves unto God, including children who resist the training they got from godly parents. Let us keep praying and keep the door open that love will tug at their hearts until God is honored in their lives, but let us be grateful that God, who has many children who have ignored him, will understand.

QUESTIONS FOR DISCUSSION

1. Do you know young couples who fear becoming parents? What are some of their concerns? How can they overcome them?
2. Which of the "time tested values" cited in the Blum study are still valid? How can they be implemented?
3. To what degree should parents today be more permissive than might have been the case in previous generations? How are greater restrictions needed?

4. Are there times when too much is expected of parents and youth today regarding their being good examples, without making any allowance for their humanity?
5. How can parents "grow" with their children? When should parents permit more independence for children?
6. Regarding "training up a child," how can parents restrict the bad influences to which their children are exposed? How can children select better friends?
7. What advice would you give to a young mother-to-be about how to care for her child in its early years?
8. Discuss heredity and child rearing? Has it been blamed too freely to excuse personal responsibility?
9. What would you say to children who bristle at reasonable restrictions placed on them by their parents or teachers? Discuss how to get them to be responsible.

12

PARENTING PAINS
BILL BAGENTS

Parenting has always been a struggle. Adam and Eve lost two sons when Cain murdered Abel (Genesis 4). Though it seems strange to say so, the loss they suffered through death may have been the easier of the two. Can you imagine their anger toward Cain—and their disappointment in him?

Noah's sons seemed to be quality men. They entered the ark with Noah and were saved from the flood. But we know that afterwards, Ham behaved improperly toward his father when Noah sinned in drunkenness (Genesis 9:18–29). Ham's sin led to a curse and a rift within the family.

Abram and Sarai faced a different kind of parenting pain. They longed for the child whom God had promised. Sarai proposed the unwise plan of having a child through her maidservant (Genesis 16). That plan led to numerous heartaches (Genesis 16:6–16 and 21:8–21).

Isaac and Rebekah created much of their own parenting pain. Genesis 25:28 tells us in a nutshell, "And Isaac loved Esau because he ate of his game, but Rebekah loved Jacob." That's a formula for trouble in any family!

Jacob married two women and had children by them — and by two more (Genesis 29:15–30:13). His family life shows us the genius of God's plan (Genesis 2:24). Jacob had both a favorite wife and a favorite son. In loving Joseph ahead of his brothers, Jacob created bitter rivalry within his own family (Genesis 37:24). This rivalry led to a murder plot, kidnapping, the selling of a brother as a slave, and the breaking of a father's heart.

Eli's failure as a parent incurred God's wrath. The Lord told young Samuel why He would be judging Eli and his family. 1 Samuel 3:13 reads, "For I have told him that I will judge his house forever for the iniquity which he knows, because his sons have made themselves vile and he did not restrain them."

Eli knew about their sin. He even confronted them (1 Samuel 2:22–25). But he would not use the power of his priestly office to make them do right. 1 Samuel 2 even indicates that Eli joined in some of their sins, particularly the sin of taking more than was authorized of the meat brought for sacrifice.

For all his strengths, David was a classic neglectful father. He knew what Amnon did to his sister, Tamar. 2 Samuel 13:21 says, "But when King David heard of all these things, he was very angry." Sadly, his anger did not lead to action. When David failed to act, Absalom did.

EASING LIFE'S HURTS

Absalom's murder of his brother was the beginning of an even greater rebellion.

CLASSIC ERRORS

In the examples listed above, we see many classic parenting errors. Such errors continue to be repeated to this day. We mention some of them in the hope that to be forewarned is to be forearmed.

Abram and Sarai tried to "improve" on God's plan of one man married to one woman for life. While we have the greatest of respect for godly single parents, we know that God's way reflects God's love. Surrogate parenting takes many forms today. None of these forms is within God's plan for the home. And, no matter what the reason, blended families face a unique set of parenting problems.

Isaac and Rebekah remind us of the grave consequences of having a favorite child. In truth, some children are better "matches" for a particular parent's personality and needs. However, each child must be loved fully and freely by each parent. Any other approach invites jealousy. Any other approach encourages discord.

Even the common practice of attempting to motivate one child by comparing him to a sibling is dangerous. And we've all heard it done. "Why can't you be more like your sister? She never gives us any trouble."

Jacob shows us another classic error. He knew the pains of favoritism within the family firsthand. Yet, he repeated the error of his father and mother by loving Joseph most.

It happens so often. When people grow up to become parents, they repeat the very behavior which harmed them as children. It takes a thoughtful person to love his own parents—"warts and all"—and to show them all due respect, while consciously refusing to repeat their parenting errors.

We often think of Eli as a man who neglected his own children for the sake of God's work. While this involves a bit of an assumption, we know that the danger is real. He failed to chasten his sons while there was hope (Proverbs 19:18). In failing to correct them, he failed to show them love (Proverbs 13:24). Eli's parenting mistakes show us the terrible end of a child who is "left to himself" (Proverbs 29:15).

David repeated this pattern of parental neglect. He withheld correction from Amnon, who was likely a teenager at the time of his terrible sin. In withholding correction, he allowed the problem to fester and worsen. Finally, he lost the ability to help or save his son (Proverbs 23:13–14).

David clearly loved his children, after a fashion. Who could forget his plea to "Deal gently for my sake with the young man Absalom" (2 Samuel 18:5)? His first question when a messenger ran from the battle was, "Is the young man Absalom safe?" (2 Samuel 18:32). His words of mourning, as recorded in 2 Samuel 18:33, are powerful and haunting.

David loved his children, after a fashion. But he failed to translate that love into daily training and supervision (Deuteronomy 6:4–9; Ephesians 6:4). We have to wonder if one reason David faced so much pain as a parent was his loss of the "moral high ground" through his own sin with Bathsheba.

GOOD EXAMPLES FROM SCRIPTURE

Thankfully, biblical examples of parenting pains do not tell the whole story. The good examples are also present, just as we would expect in such a balanced book. Just as we would also expect, some of the good examples come from some of the people who made their share of mistakes.

To their credit, Abraham and Sarah instilled faith in their son. Isaac showed tremendous respect for his father during that fateful trip to Mount Moriah (Genesis 22). He allowed his father to bind him to the altar. Once delivered, he continued to embrace the promise which God had made to his father (Hebrews 11:8–16). Isaac's son, Jacob, embraced this promise as well.

Despite their error regarding Hagar, Abraham and Sarah proved effective parents. The Lord's plan, as stated in Genesis 18:19, bore fruit. Abraham did "command his children and his household after him that they keep the way of the Lord, to do righteousness and justice, that the Lord may bring to Abraham what He has spoken to him."

Though Isaac and Rebekah made the classic mistake of each having a favorite child, the brothers somehow "outgrew" their rivalry. Genesis 31–33 shows us that God had a hand in their healing.

As Jacob and his entourage were returning, his fear grew as he approached his homeland. He even divided his caravan into two parts saying, "If Esau comes to the one company and attacks it, then the other company which is left will escape" (Genesis 32:8). He asked God for protection (Genesis 32:9–12). He sent impressive presents ahead to Esau, hoping to prepare for a peaceful meeting (Genesis 32:13–21). Still, Esau's warm greeting must have surprised him (Genesis 33:4)!

The reunion of these brothers reminds us that no one is a prisoner of childrearing hurts. Though these brothers were wronged and wounded by their parents' favoritism, they were not doomed by it. The concept of perpetual victimhood is a modern and errant idea. Ezekiel 18 clearly demonstrates that ungodly parents do not guarantee ungodly children. Sadly, the opposite is also true: godly parents do not unconditionally guarantee godly children. Individual responsibility always plays a role.

We rightly uphold God's plan that both parents should work together as a team in parenting. We see the wisdom of what some have described as "parenting in stereo." At the same time, we know this is not always the case. One of the most outstanding biblical examples of good parenting is that of Lois and Eunice (2 Timothy 1:3–5). Timothy knew the Holy Scriptures from childhood, because his mother and grandmother taught him (2 Timothy 3:14–15).

Though Eunice was married to a Gentile, who was almost certainly an unbeliever, she enlisted the help of her mother to provide a unique version of "parenting in stereo" (Acts 16:1–5). These ladies offer strong encouragement to those who must parent without full unity today. Even under less than ideal conditions, faith can still be instilled. Even when one parent chooses not to help, it is still powerful and right to teach God's word to children.

The concept of multigenerational teaching, of involving grandparents in the rearing of children, is well-supported by Scripture. Deuteronomy 4:9–14 urges parents to keep God's commandments "and teach them to your children and your grandchildren." Deuteronomy 6:1–9 makes the same point. Judges 2:7–10 and the chapters which follow document the tragedy which results from failing to follow God's plan for parenting.

WHY DON'T MORE PARENTS DO BETTER?

We begin with the assumption that most parents truly love their children. We have biblical documentation of the terrible effects of bad parenting. We have biblical proof that good parenting is possible. Why, then, don't more parents—especially Christian parents—do a better job of parenting?

It has been said that most parents do just about as well as they know to do. When thinking of Christian parents, this statement may be true. Children don't come with an instruction manual. Most couples have no formal training in parenting. Titus 2:1–10 tends to be neglected, even within the church. When it comes to parenting skills, most of us know only what we learned from our experience with our own parents.

Of course, these statements have numerous implications for the local church. Many childrearing hurts could be lessened or prevented by:

- Offering parenting courses on various levels. i.e., preparing for parenting, parenting toddlers, parenting during the elementary years, parenting teens, and transitioning from a parent-child to an adult-adult relationship with your children.
- Offering courses within the Bible school program in which older women teach younger women.
- Presenting sermon series which deal with basic parenting principles from a biblical perspective.
- Adding a parenting resource section to the church library.
- Creating a parenting-skills newsletter or a parenting section of the weekly church bulletin.
- The statements above also have implications for individual families.
- Couples can explore the similarities, differences, strengths, and weaknesses in the childrearing styles of their respective parents.
- Couples can choose to read (advisedly) from the vast literature of parenting.
- Couples can study together from the great parenting texts of Scripture (Deuteronomy 4 & 6; Proverbs 31; Ephesians 6:1–4), giving

special attention to application within their own family.
- Young couples can seek the counsel and wisdom of older couples, especially those who have earned respect as strong parents.

Many Christian parents may not be doing a better job of childrearing primarily because of a lack of knowledge. Others may be overly influenced by modern parenting theories. For example, the current politically correct concept of childrearing confidently prohibits spanking. Perhaps you have heard the following slogans: "Violence begets violence" and "Hitting teaches hitting."

Clearly, we would neither condone nor excuse physical abuse. We know that corrective discipline is only one aspect—and, by definition, the smaller aspect—of training our children. At the same time, we must not ignore the teaching of Scripture. Corrective discipline has its place (Proverbs 9:18, 22:15, and 23:13–14). Proverbs 13:24 identifies corrective discipline as a proof of parental love. Proverbs 29:15 reminds us that a lack of corrective discipline is, itself, a form of parental neglect.

In keeping with Proverbs 17:10, loving parents prefer to correct their children with words. Wise parents teach at all times. At the same time, there are cases when words alone are insufficient. To do what's best, even when we feel like doing less, will spare us a world of childrearing hurt.

Some parents seem to have adopted the modern notion that children are miniature adults and should be treated as such. While children should not be bullied or disrespected, they are not miniature adults. There is considerable foolishness and immaturity within their childish ways (Proverbs 22:15; 1 Corinthians 13:11; Ephesians 4:11–16). In every healthy home, the parents realize that they are the adults. And, they act accordingly.

Some parents seem to believe that children—even very young children—should be allowed to make their own decisions. However, this concept is inconsistently applied. Parents who argue, "We shouldn't make our children attend Bible class. After all, that could turn them against God for life ..." will not apply the same reasoning in allowing their children to skip school.

Godly parents are not over-controlling. It's not in their hearts to micromanage their children. To do so would be to invite the twin hurts of impeding their development and provoking them to discouragement (Colossians 3:21). At the same time, godly parents know how accurately to answer the famous question, "Who's the adult here?" They do not abdicate their God-given authority and responsibility.

Some parents seem to believe that their children should learn only what they intentionally teach. In the more radical version, perhaps some parents believe that their children do learn only what they purposefully teach. Scripture clearly urges parents to be constant intentional teachers (Deuteronomy 6:4–9). Yet, even Deuteronomy 6 begins by encouraging parents (and others) to fear and obey the Lord.

Children learn by nature. They soak in information like sponges. They may learn even more efficiently when we are not intentionally teaching them. Every wise parent knows that, when it comes to learning, children don't have an off switch. The only way to teach them consistently well is to live consistently well before them.

Why don't more parents do a better job of rearing their children? One final reason may be more honest and to the point than all those listed above. Childrearing is time consuming hard work! It takes sacrificial devotion to do a good job. But, doing a good job of parenting is worth the time and the work. Not only will it spare so many so much pain, it also blesses countless lives with joy.

DISCLAIMER

There are no perfect parents. Perhaps the best parents are those who are most aware of their own imperfections. Even if there were perfect parents, parents are far from the only influence in their children's lives. Even if there were perfect parents, no power under heaven can take away a child's right to choose his own attitude and conduct.

Even the best parents cannot guarantee the faithfulness of their children. Even the worst parents cannot doom their children to destruction. Even parents who were not faithful during their children's most formative years are not without recourse. It is never too late to begin walking with God. While life lasts, it is never too late to change our influence and example. Every step that we take toward Jesus is a step in the right direction.

QUESTIONS FOR DISCUSSION

1. In your judgment, is parenting more of a struggle today than in years past? Give reasons for your answer.
2. Why does Scripture give so many examples of parenting pain?
3. Why are we so consistent in repeating the mistakes of our parents as we work to rear our children?
4. In thinking of Eli in 1 Samuel 1–4, why did he allow his sons to sin so grievously?
5. Does 1 Samuel 8:1–5 indicate that Samuel repeated Eli's parenting errors? Give reasons for your answer.
6. What modern trends do you view as most harmful to effective childrearing?
7. Do you believe most parents feel too much responsibility for their children? Too little? Explain.

13

HURTS CAUSED BY THINGS

JACK P. WILHELM

We have studied mostly about hurts that are people caused. Sometimes our hurts are caused by things. Jesus did a lot of teaching about "things." He taught us that life does not consist of the "abundance of things which one possesses" (Luke 12:15).

Paul warned of the hurts that things can bring to us:

> Those who desire to be rich fall into temptation and a snare, and into many foolish and harmful lusts which drown men in destruction and perdition. For the love of money is a root of all kinds of evil, for which some have strayed from the faith in their greediness, and pierced themselves through with many sorrows. (1 Timothy 6:9-11).

IS PROSPERITY ALWAYS WRONG?

A word of caution is needed here. The Bible is not condemning prosperity. If prosperity is obtained honorably and used wisely, it has God's approval. As a matter of fact, it will come from him! One of the first things God wanted his people to understand when he brought them out of Egyptian bondage was that "you shall remember the Lord your God, for it is he who gives you power to get wealth, that he may establish his covenant" (Deuteronomy 8:18).

John prayed that his good friend Gaius might "prosper in all things and be in health, even as your soul prospers" (3 John 2). Prosperity comes from God. It may not come as rapidly as we desire, and we may not always know how to calculate what real prosperity is, but it is almost unavoidable. We do not always use the same guidelines for determining who is "rich." The "rich" person may be the one who has a few more of this world's creature comforts than we have.

Two little children were canvassing their neighborhood, asking for old newspapers they could sell to help their mother meet expenses. It was a cold day and they appeared chilled, so a kind lady invited them inside her home and served them some hot chocolate while she gathered some papers to give them. One of them said, "Lady, are you rich?"

She chuckled, because she had never thought of her modest circumstances as making her rich. She said, "No. What would make you think that?"

EASING LIFE'S HURTS

The child replied, "Because all your cups have handles."

Some of us may well remember using dishes that were certainly not matched sets in childhood and we had other living conditions that would qualify us today as living in poverty. But we never thought that we were below the poverty level as long as there was love and adequate food to eat.

Being "rich" is a relative term. The street person who hovers in a cardboard box over a heating grate on a busy street may think that another homeless person who has a sleeping bag is rich. That person who still has to forage through dumpsters may think that one who gets food stamps is rich. That person thinks that a man who can take his family to a fast food restaurant is rich. The McDonald's patron though thinks that a man who could order a steak when he eats out is rich. Further down the line, the man who can take his family on a vacation is rich, but not, he thinks, compared to one who can buy a new van to take the trip in. And to one who gets the new van, the fellow who can fill its gas tank is rich! They all envy the man who can take a cruise, but the cruiser envies the fellow who owns his own yacht and can travel in it around the world.

Elsewhere in the lineup, the "poor" sports fan who can attend one game a year regards the one who can buy season tickets for his favorite team as "rich." But the season ticket holder thinks the man who can shell out $50,000 annually for a plush box in the new Dome is rich. The box occupant though regards the rich person as one who can always buy his new wife a million-dollar diamond ring and a multimillion-dollar home. It's all relative, isn't it?

PROBLEMS CONFRONTING THE RICH

We forget that the rich at every level have hurts and problems. I remember hearing the newsman David Brinkley speak at a school function. He told of a wealthy heiress who happened to ask him at a social function what time it was so she could set her watch. She said, "They forgot to wind my watch this morning." He said, "The rich do have problems, you know." Someone has said that if you are poor, your faults are proof that you are an uncouth clod; if you are rich, your faults simply mean that you are eccentric.

A Beverly Hills, California, teacher once got this note explaining the absence of one of her students the day before: "Cathy couldn't come to school yesterday because we had a power failure and the electric gate wouldn't open."

It reminded me of an excuse one of my former students received after she became a teacher in a Texas school. One of her students did not have his homework, but he had an excuse: "The Dallas Cowboys played in Miami this weekend. Our big plane was in the shop and we had to take our slower little plane which made us so late getting back home, I didn't have time to do my homework."

DO WE ENVY THE RICH OR DO THEY ENVY OUR CONTENTMENT?

One of the things that sometimes hurts us is our envy of the rich. Yet they may well be among the more miserable people in the world if all they have is money. The world's first billionaire, John D. Rockefeller, said, "I can think of nothing less pleasurable than a life devoted to pleasure."

Someone has said, "If a man is not content in the state he is in, he will not be content in the state he would like to be in." Paul improved his state when he could, as when he had the hired dwelling rather than a prison cell in Rome, but he also had learned contentment. He said, "I have learned in whatever state I am, to be content," (Philippians 4:11).

A man overheard his maid say, "If I just had $20, I would really be content!" He gave it to her. As he left, he heard her mumble to herself, "Why didn't I say $50?'"

The problem of evaluating our circumstances carefully to avoid boomerang hurts must have been around for centuries. The following verses from Proverbs reflect the wisdom someone was trying to preach to the restless "boomers" of that ancient day:

Two things I request of you (deprive me not before I die): Remove falsehood and lies far from me; [and] Give me neither poverty nor riches—Feed me with the food you prescribe for me lest I be full and deny you, and say, "Who is the Lord?' or lest I be poor and steal, and profane the name of my God. (Proverbs 30:7–9).

You see risks associated with things: If we have too

much, we may say, "Who needs the Lord?" If we have too little, we may get bitter and turn against God.

SOME WAYS THAT "THINGS" CAUSE HURT

Sometimes "things" bring us hurt because we let them enslave us with an unhealthy spirit of greed Solomon was the guinea pig for the whole human family. Nothing was withheld that his eyes desired, but there was still an emptiness in his life. He warned about the hurt of insatiable greed:

He who loves silver will not be satisfied with silver; nor he who loves abundance, with increase. This is vanity. When goods increase, they increase who eat them, so what profit have the owners except to see them with their eyes? The sleep of a laboring man is sweet, whether he eats little or much, but the abundance of the rich will not permit him to sleep. There is a severe evil I have seen under the sun; riches kept for their owner to his hurt (Ecclesiastes 5:10–13).

I recall once visiting with five different millionaires within a one-month period. They all seemed to be burdened with their wealth. One of them was the one I mentioned earlier who told me he had already reached the point that he could not sleep at night because of pressures connected with managing his estate. All of them were giving some thought to making plans to let some of their possessions be used for charitable works when they did not need them anymore. All have now passed on, and of the five, only one man and his wife followed through with any provision to do that—and they were the only ones of the group who were not Christians. Sometimes it hurts people to part with their possessions. Like Nabal, it petrifies them to lose control (1 Samuel 25).

God warned the Israelites that a greedy, disobedient spirit would bring hurts back to them: their crops would be unproductive, their land and families would be ravished by others, and "the alien who is among you shall rise higher and higher above you, and you shall become lower and lower because you did not serve the Lord your God with joy and gladness of heart, for the abundance of things ..." (Deuteronomy 28:43, 47).

If you have ever seen greedy dogs snap and devour each other as they fight over morsels of food, even attacking the hand that feeds them, you will see special meaning in Isaiah 56:11: "Yes, they are greedy dogs which never have enough." The greedy person always gets what he wants, but never enough of it! It hurts him or her to know that something is in reach which they have not yet been able to grasp.

Sometimes "things'" hurt because we are depending on them to do something which they were never intended to do. We would like for our "things" to satisfy us, to secure us, to liberate us from duty, and to elevate our stature with God and others. We think that would "really be living."

A man made plans to be buried in his old faithful T-Model Ford automobile. When that time came, as people watched the procedure of the car being lowered into the grave with its owner in it, one of them exclaimed, "Man, that's what I call really livin'!" But

Jesus makes it clear that it takes more than something like that to be living. He said, "One's life does not consist in the abundance of the things which he possesses."

Paul taught us that "we brought nothing [no thing] into this world, and it is certain we can carry nothing [no thing] out" (1 Timothy 6:7). In the same context, he warned "those who desire to be rich" (v. 9) "not to be haughty, nor to trust in uncertain riches but in the living God, who gives us richly all things to enjoy" (v. 17). Jesus said there is a "deceitfulness of riches" (Matthew 13:22). Riches make us think we are secure if we have laid up treasures on earth (Matthew 6:19-21), but they are deceptive. The "true riches" (Luke 16:11) are given only to those who are faithful to God's other requirements.

Read Proverbs 11:28: "He who trusts in his riches will fall, but the righteous will flourish like foliage." Jesus taught us this when he spoke of the rich fool in Luke 12 who thought he was secure for the future because of his bounty. His soul, which was spiritual, could not be nourished on things, which are temporal. The time may come when one would give a thousand worlds like this one for the one thing overlooked in our search for pleasure.

Sometimes things happen that remind us that life is more precious than money. The *Birmingham News* (Jan. 30, 1990) carried the story of two lost skiers who decided "they had money to burn." It was a decision that saved their lives. They had strayed out of the bounds of a resort and were lost. More than 30 searchers set out in waist deep snow shortly after dark to find them. They burned their currency to create a fire and smoke which led to their rescue. They decided that life was worth more than money.

I will admit that it hurts just a bit to think of all those five, ten, twenty, or fifty-dollar bills being burned, but that was better than not being rescued. I related that story once in a sermon and added, "I think I would have torn those bills so that I could burn only the short ends first, because if you have over half of a torn bill, you can get it replaced at a bank. Maybe they could have been rescued before they had to burn the longer ends of the bills." One of the elders in the crowd came up afterwards and said, "I have a better idea. I would have just written checks and burned them!" (Now you know how elders think!)

Sometimes "things" bring us hurts because of the way they are used. There is the matter of abuse. The prodigal son left home with his pockets literally bulging with resources. He had thrown off the restraints of his father, but he had no self-restraint and he "wasted his possessions with prodigal living" (Luke 15:13). His older brother later accused him of "devouring his livelihood with harlots" (v. 30). The charge wasn't denied, but we are not told in detail just how the abuse of his resources resulted in the waste. Perhaps the older brother was merely thinking of what he would have done had he been in his place. The younger son at least learned that a lot more people will help you sin and become impoverished than will help you get back on your feet. He had to retrace his steps to find forgiveness and rehabilitation.

Most good Christian people though will probably not have this experience. For us, it will be more a matter of misuse of our things rather than abuse. Misuse can occur even in the pursuit of things that are ordinarily not wrong in themselves. The rich fool in Luke 12 was not condemned because he built his bigger barns to care for his prosperity. Had he let his crops lie wasting in the field, that would have been wrong. His problem was that he did not include God in his plans and thought his soul could be nourished on the material things.

The evangelist T. B. Larimore once traveled overnight by train to get to a preaching appointment. A brother met the train and was surprised that Larimore did not get off of the coach when the train came in. He looked near the end of the train and saw Larimore getting off of the Pullman car. The man said, "Brother Larimore, I'm surprised that you slept in the Pullman car. You could have ridden in the coach and saved the Lord's money."

Brother Larimore said, "I decided to sleep in the Pullman and save the Lord's servant." Sometimes there is a question of what is "fair use" of our possessions, but there is also a "false economy" that may be more costly than the "waste." Jesus tried to tell us that. When some criticized the woman, who anointed him with "an alabaster flask of very costly oil of spikenard" he said, "Let her alone! Why do you trouble her? She has done a good work for me" (Mark 14:3–9). They had not been denied an opportunity to do good because of what she was doing. The further we get away from covetousness, the less quibbling we hear about generous support of good works. It's the abuse for things that are not worthy that we need to evaluate more carefully.

There is also the hurt that is connected with disuse of our resources. We are tempted to "lay up treasures on earth" rather than use them in a way that will help us be received "into everlasting habitations." The one talent man illustrated for us that it is not enough to "hold our own." He was told that he "ought to have deposited my money with the bankers, and at my coming, I would have received back my own with interest," (Matthew 25:27). Don't misunderstand this. No one is saying that we can buy God off or that the church is merely to be in the banking business. At the same time, the matter of our financial accountability will come up at the judgment. James 5 puts that in focus. Resources that indicate disuse because they are "corrupted ... motheaten ... corroded, ... will be a witness against you..." (James 5:1–3). If we "weep and howl for your miseries that are coming upon you" (v. 1), there will be some hurts that are caused by disuse as much as by abuse or misuse.

A man once converted most of his assets into a beautiful diamond. He didn't trust banks. He feared inflation. He feared theft. He thought his diamond would be a safe hedge, provided he could hide it in a secure place. He located what he thought was a secluded place and hid it under a rock. He found pleasure and reassurance by sneaking away regularly to lift up the rock and see that his valuable diamond was still there.

He did that so frequently that a thief saw him and wondered what he was doing. The thief followed him, noticed where the rock and diamond were, and after he left, stole the diamond. The next time the man went, he discovered that his diamond was missing and panicked.

He told one of his friends what had happened. His friend gave him a pebble and said, "Why don't you take this pebble and put it under the rock in place of the diamond?"

The man said, "What good would that do? It wouldn't be my diamond. That pebble has no value!"

His friend said, "Yes, but if you have no plans to use the diamond, one rock is as good as another!"

QUESTIONS FOR DISCUSSION

1. Read 1 Timothy 6:10. What would you say to one who refers to this passage and says, "Money is the root of all evil?"
2. What comes to your mind when you hear, "A higher percentage of the wealthiest people in the world live in America, more than anywhere else in the world?"
3. What will help a rich person to avoid thinking that he does not need God if he is economically sufficient?
4. What will help one who is poor to avoid becoming bitter toward God and people who have been blessed more than he/she has been blessed?
5. Is it wrong for a person to desire—even pray—for his lot in life to be improved and enriched?
6. Elaborate on the statement Jesus made about the "deceitfulness of riches." What is

deceptive about them? How can one "take heed that he not be deceived" by them?
7. Which is more serious for most of us—the abuse, the misuse, or the disuse of our resources?
8. Read Luke 16:9. How can one "make friends for yourselves by unrighteous mammon, that when you fail, they may receive you into everlasting habitation"?

14

OUR ATTITUDE TOWARD MONEY
BILL BAGENTS

You know how much our culture values wealth. People are often judged on the basis of their income or net worth. The poor, if not despised, are at least looked down upon. You know what people say about money.

- Money makes the world go around.
- You can never be too rich or too thin.
- Money never goes out of style.
- In America, anyone who sets his mind to it can be rich.

In our wiser moments, we know that money is just a tool. Money is morally neutral, neither good nor evil in and of itself. It was God who blessed Abraham and Solomon with riches (Genesis 14:21–24; 1 Kings 3:1–15). It was God who restored and increased the riches of Job (Job 42:12).

While material wealth can be a blessing from God, we also know that money can be dangerous. 1 Timothy 6:9–10 are chilling verses. "But those who desire to be rich fall into temptation and a snare, and into many foolish and harmful lusts which drown men in destruction and perdition. For the love of money is a root of all kinds of evil, for which some have strayed from the faith in their greediness and pierced themselves through with many sorrows."

Scripture offers many examples of those who "pierced themselves" with many sorrows through the love of money.

- The love of money led Lot to choose the fertile plain and pitch his tent toward Sodom (Genesis 13).
- The love of money led Achan to steal, in direct violation of God's command (Joshua 7).
- The love of money led Gehazi to lie to Naaman and Elisha (2 Kings 5:20–27).
- The love of money seems to have been one reason that Ananias and Sapphira lied to God (Acts 5:1–11).

First Timothy 6:3–21 identifies many dangerous attitudes related to wealth. These attitudes set people up for the sorrows described in verses 9 and 10. Consider the following:

- Verse 5, some see godliness as a means of material gain.

- Verses 6–8, some have an attitude toward material wealth which robs them of contentment.
- Verse 7, some so value wealth that they forget that we can't take it with us.
- Verse 9, the desire to be rich easily leads people into temptation.
- Verse 10, the love of money quickly grows into greed which leads people away from the faith.
- Verse 17, riches can lead to a haughtiness.
- Verse 17, those who are rich may be tempted to trust in their riches rather than trusting in God.
- Verses 18–19, those who are rich may be tempted to forget the importance of being "rich in good works."

Proverbs 23:6–8 continues the warning. Love of money can also lead to the misery of miserliness. The miser is too busy accumulating things to ever enjoy them. He can't know the blessing of giving. It's not in his heart to share. He doesn't have riches; they have him!

WHAT MONEY CAN'T BUY

As powerful as material wealth can be, we know that there are things which money cannot buy.

Money can't buy salvation. The rich man of Luke 16:19–31 proves that. The rich man took nothing to Hades with him. The fact that he had been rich couldn't buy him even one drop of water. We remember the Lord's great question of Luke 9:25, "For what advantage is it to a man if he gains the whole world, and is himself destroyed or lost?" The rich man of Luke 16 experienced the answer to Jesus' question.

While being rich can't save us, it can certainly make our salvation more difficult. During Jesus' earthly ministry, "the common people heard Him gladly" (Mark 12:37). We all know the famous words of Luke 18:24-25, "How hard it is for those who have riches to enter the kingdom of God! For it is easier for a camel to go through the eye of a needle than for a rich man to enter the kingdom of God."

Contrary to the expectation of so many, money can't buy happiness. Wealth is one thing; contentment is another (1 Timothy 6:3-10). Solomon states this fact directly. Ecclesiastes 5:10-11 reads, "He who loves silver will not be satisfied with silver; nor he who loves abundance with increase. This is also vanity. When goods increase, they increase who eat them; so, what profit have the owners except to see them with their eyes?"

Perhaps you have known rich people who were far less than happy. It's like the carrot that's tied in front of a horse. It may make him run and it may make him stretch. But, no matter how hard he tries, he can never reach it. As strange as it may sound, riches and misery are not a rare combination.

Money can't buy security. Proverbs 23:4-5 offers sound counsel, "Do not overwork to be rich: because of your own understanding, cease! Will you set your eyes on that which is not? For riches certainly make themselves wings; they fly away like an eagle toward heaven." As some have noted, either they fly away or we do. Either way, riches don't last. We cannot find peace of mind in things which don't last.

Contrary to the promise of this world, money can't buy self-worth. There is great danger in reckoning our worth in terms of material wealth. Luke 12:15 is clear: "Take heed and beware of covetousness, for one's life does not consist in the abundance of the things he possesses." Those words are so true!

Even those who don't know God do know that there's more to us than our net worth. Net worth rises and falls with the next turn in the market. Some have a knack for making money. Some inherit wealth. Some, like Job, lose all they have due to no fault of their own. Money has never been the source of our worth (Genesis 1:26–27).

Perhaps it should go without saying that money can't buy love. Even what appears to be sacrificial love is nothing unless it is accompanied by the attitude of love (1 Corinthians 13:1–3). True love flows from the heart. It can't be bought and sold.

Even trying to buy love is a set-up for disappointment. Have you ever known a parent who tried to substitute things for time with his children? As the children grow older, the things grow bigger (more expensive). But, often, so does the resentment. Relationships aren't built on dollar value. Our hearts trade only in the currency of love.

EXTREMES BEGET EXTREMES

In emphasizing what money can't buy, we dare not declare money the ultimate evil. Some seem to have done so. Out of fear of the love of money, they flee to the opposite extreme of glorifying poverty.

Being rich can't save us, but neither can being poor. It is clear that God loves the poor. Proverbs 14:31 reads, "He who oppresses the poor reproaches his Maker, but he who honors him has mercy on the needy." When John's disciples needed proof that Jesus was the Messiah, part of the evidence which Jesus offered to them was that "... the poor have the gospel preached to them" (Luke 7:22). Jesus Himself was among the poor during His earthly life.

Despite these great truths, poverty has no saving power. Being poor, in fact, presents its own unique set of temptations. We appreciate the balance of Proverbs 30:7-9, " ... Give me neither poverty nor riches—feed me with the food You prescribe for me; lest I be full and deny You, and say, 'Who is the Lord?' or lest I be poor and steal, and profane the name of my God."

Neither wealth nor poverty can, in and of themselves, cause anyone to be either saved or lost. This we can affirm with confidence: Our attitude toward money is far more important than its absence or abundance in our lives. An ungodly attitude toward money is a setup for sorrow.

Some believe that wealth is always a sign of God's favor. In its strong form, this belief asserts, "If I'm financially successful, then I must be right with God." This is a common approach to easing life's hurts for those in the world's richest nations. It gives people permission to declare themselves safe and saved. Such thinking is without biblical merit.

At the opposite extreme, some believe that poverty is a sign of God's favor. Luke 6:20 does teach, "Blessed are you poor, for yours is the kingdom of God." However, we dare not forget that Scripture also identifies poor management, selfishness, and laziness as causes of poverty in some cases (Proverbs 6:6–11, 10:4–5, 11:24–26, 24:30–34). In Isaiah 1:7–9, the cause of the pain and poverty which the prophet predicted was God's judgment of the people's sins.

POVERTY AND WEALTH: ISSUES WITHIN THE CHURCH

Attitudes toward poverty and wealth have impact even beyond the personal and family levels. They also affect our fellowship in Christ. James 2:1–13 strongly warns against showing economic partiality within the body of Christ. Such partiality is clearly sinful (James 2:9).

This world makes great distinction between the "haves" and the "have nots." We understand that these broad categories are highly relative and situation dependent. A family with a $50,000 annual income will be a "have" when compared to a family with half that income. It may well be a "have not" when compared to a family in the six-figure range.

Satan is wise in his work. He realizes the power of natural divisions. He will exploit those divisions to cause pain to God's people and harm to the body of Christ. He will tempt us to do just what is discussed in James 2.

The setting is the worship assembly. Two visitors attend. One is obviously "well to do." We know that from the gold rings and the fine clothing. He has success written all over him. He is warmly welcomed and shown to a prominent seat.

The other visitor is just as obviously poor. We are not told why. Perhaps he has been mistreated by others. Perhaps he has little "business sense." Maybe he grew up in a difficult home and was not taught the values which make for economic success. Maybe his health has limited his ability to work. Whatever the case, he is poor. And, he is treated poorly because of that (James 2:3b).

Satan can use such partiality against the church. Satan will use such partiality against us. He will tempt the rich man to think, "I'm somebody! My riches entitle me to special status and treatment. I should have a big voice in the affairs of this church."

The poor man will also be tempted. He could be tempted to think, "These folks think they're too good for me. If they don't want me here, then I don't have to be here." Oppositely, he could reason, "I'm not good enough for God to love me. Even God's people know that He has no place for me."

The devil doesn't care which direction he pushes, as long as he pushes people away from God. He doesn't care how he hurts people, as long as they do not turn to God for relief. It has been said, "The devil doesn't care which ditch he pushes people into. He just wants them off the road."

Satan would love to help people believe that the rich and the poor can never get along. If they can't get along, surely, they can't worship together. Discord and division are his business. He's the master of separation. He must be opposed!

PRACTICAL SUGGESTIONS

What's the answer to these temptations? How can we keep Satan from using hurts over poverty and affluence to harm the body of Christ? We offer the following suggestions:

- Remember that any wealth we "possess" is a gift from God. It would be ungrateful to feel guilty because God has blessed us.
- Remember that, in truth, we never possess anything. Whatever we seem to have is really "on loan" from God. We should use it to His glory.
- Remember that God does not judge us based on our material assets. If God does not make money His criterion for assessment, then we shouldn't either.
- If we are among the more blessed, financially speaking, then we must resist the temptation to flaunt our wealth. To do so would insult those who have less. Even in acts of benevolence, Jesus teaches us not to let our

left hand know what our right hand is doing (Matthew 6:1-4).
- If we are among the less blessed, financially speaking, then we must resist the temptations of jealousy and envy. Both of these sins are among the obvious works of the flesh (Galatians 5:19-21).
- If rich, we must never oppress the poor (James 2:6-7).
- If poor, we must not underestimate our ability to give to God. Attitude, not amount, determines the greatness of the gift. In the famous case of the widow's two mites, Jesus was observing how, not how much, people gave (Mark 12:41). The Macedonians did not let their poverty rob them of the joy and grace of giving (2 Corinthians 8:1-7).

We see so many who are hurt by the love of money. It seems that this world is growing increasingly materialistic. How can we fight this trend? How can we spare ourselves the sorrow which the love of money causes?

Matthew 22:34-40 holds one answer. We can love God with all our heart, soul, and mind. We can love our neighbors as ourselves. In doing so, we will always love truth more than money. We will always love people more than things.

Second Corinthians 9:7 holds another answer. "... God loves a cheerful giver." The cheerful giver knows the truth of Acts 20:35. He welcomes the blessing of giving in the name of Christ and to the glory of God.

Money can't control him because God is already in control of his life.

QUESTIONS FOR DISCUSSION

1. In your judgment, which causes more of life's hurts, poverty or affluence? Why?
2. Why is it so tempting to trust in riches?
3. Why is it so tempting to judge ourselves (and others) in light of net worth?
4. Why do people tend to credit themselves with financial prosperity, but to blame others for financial problems?
5. Are the poor really more receptive to the gospel? Explain.
6. Do issues of poverty and affluence still cause harm to the body of Christ?
7. How can I tell if I love money too much? What will show that I am a victim of the love of money?

15

CAREER JOLTS
BILL BAGENTS

As each new generation looks back, some aspects of life seem simpler and easier. This is especially true in the area of one's vocation. Once, sons almost always followed in their fathers' footsteps. "What do you want to be when you grow up?" was an unimaginable question. When it came to choosing his life's work, he would be what his father and his grandfather were. But we live in an age of tremendous freedom and excessive choice.

It's not just the freedom to choose that has changed. Once, a man went to work with a company and stayed with that company until he retired. Today we live in a world of buyouts, mergers, and hostile takeovers. Older workers, many of whom are not old at all, are phased out to make way for "young blood." Entire plants close to move their operation overseas. New technology renders some jobs obsolete.

Now men and women alike know the trauma of

career jolts. For some, it's "take the promotion and move across the country or start looking for another place to work." Companies don't tend to think of children in school or your spouse's job. For some, the hurt is being passed over for promotion due to quotas or differing quantities of formal education. For some, it's "stay on the career track and neglect your family or get off that track and take your chances." Negative scenarios abound. Not everyone enjoys a golden parachute.

THE BIBLE'S HIGH VIEW OF WORK

Scripture takes a high view of work. Many wrongly assume that the need to work was part of the punishment for Adam's sin. They forget Genesis 2:15: "Then the Lord took the man and put him in the garden of Eden to tend and keep it." The naming of the animals and birds could be considered work as well (Genesis 2:19–20). God blessed Adam with that work before any human had sinned.

It is certainly correct to say that work became more difficult because of sin (Genesis 3:17–19). It is certainly wrong to say that work exists because of sin. Ecclesiastes 2:24 reads, "There is nothing better for a man than that he should eat and drink, and that his soul should enjoy good in his labor. This also, I saw, was from the hand of God."

Honest work is a blessing of God. Hard work contributed notably to the stellar reputation of the worthy woman of Proverbs 31. Her lamp did not go out at night. She worked willingly with her hands. The chapter ends with high praise: "Give her the fruit of her hands, and let her own works praise her in the gates."

Thankfully, neither the value of our work nor the ability of work to bless our lives depends on the virtue of our employer. Paul reminded Titus that even slaves could "adorn the doctrine of God our Savior" working honestly, respectfully, and obediently (Titus 2:9–10). As negative and damaging as slavery could be, it could not take away the dignity of hard work.

Paul explains the dynamic behind Titus 2:9–10 in Colossians 3:22–24. "Servants, obey in all things your masters according to the flesh, not with eye-service as men-pleasers, but in sincerity of heart, fearing God. And whatever you do, do it heartily as to the Lord and not to men, knowing that from the Lord you will receive the reward of the inheritance; for you serve the Lord Christ." Again, the original context was the master-slave relationship. We are blessed to be able to apply these principles in the employer-employee relationship.

Christians work honestly. Christians work hard. We are model employees because of our respect for God. We can put our hearts into any honest work. By doing so, we obey the Lord and provide for our families. By doing so, even when conditions are unfair, we refuse to be overcome by evil and choose to overcome evil with good (Romans 12:21). By doing so, we demonstrate trust in God. We show the world our confidence in God. Our actions tell the world that God will make things right.

Scripture has a high view of work. From our human perspective, we think of the apostle Paul as a great man. He stands as a powerful example of faith. We know that he filled his God-ordained role as "a chosen vessel" to bear God's name before the Gentiles (Acts 9:15). Yet, God frequently allowed Paul to support both himself and his fellow workers with the work of his own hands (Acts 18:1–3 and 20:34; 2 Corinthians 12:11–21, 1 Thessalonians 2:1–12; 2 Thessalonians 3:6–10).

Why did the Lord allow Paul to do what we sometimes call "secular work"? It was not that the preaching of the gospel failed to provide plenty of challenges. It was not that Paul somehow had no right to receive the help of brethren. It was not that Paul needed a second career. I believe that part of the reason was to warn us against the fallacy of dividing work into "secular work" and "church work." No matter what work we are doing at the moment, it is always our purpose to bring glory to God.

GOD'S USE OF OUR WORK

Scripture documents how the Lord has used a good work ethic to advance His servants. Rebekah's respect and willing work caught the eye of Abraham's servant (Genesis 24). The way she worked contributed to her becoming the bride of Isaac and an ancestor of Jesus Christ. Joseph's work elevated him within Potiphar's house (Genesis 39). Though a false accusation cost him that job, the skills gained on that job may have helped prepare him to save God's people from famine. Daniel's faithful work, specifically the excellent spirit that was in him, elevated him above every other ruler whom Darius appointed (Daniel 6).

Of course, Daniel's success had a backlash. It stirred the jealousy of others, leading Daniel to the lions' den. But we know God's vindication of Daniel. The accusers were the ones crushed by the lions.

How does God use our work today? No doubt, you can add to the following list.

- God uses work to teach us responsibility and discipline.
- God uses work to put us in close daily contact with those who need the gospel.
- God uses work, especially its uncertainties, to help us know that we need to trust Him.
- God uses work, especially its unfairness and frustration, to help us realize that we need to cast our cares on Him (1 Peter 5:5–7).
- God uses work as a means by which we uphold the faith by providing for our families (1 Timothy 5:8).
- God uses work as a means of keeping us emotionally and psychologically healthy. Those who find meaning in their work live longer, happier, and healthier lives.

WHEN CAREER JOLTS COME

Despite the Bible's high view of work and the many ways God uses work to bless us, career jolts still come. Studies of midlife crises consistently include job-related issues among the many "causes." Some people find themselves in "dead end" jobs. Others finally realize that they are not meeting the lofty dreams of great careers that motivated them in their youth. As they look at their jobs and at their lives as a whole, they ask themselves, "Is this all there is?"

There is a strong tendency in our culture to define our lives in terms of our careers. Many years ago, a lady asked my mother if she thought she had let herself down by choosing to be a career homemaker. Truthfully, I think she was chiding mom for letting herself down by failing to "realize her potential" within the workplace.

Mom was never without work. Six children provided plenty of challenge. We were blessed to be able to live on the money that Dad brought in. Even that would not have been possible without Mom's management and effort.

Mom answered the lady in terms of six healthy, growing, Christian children. To this day, none of us are in jail. All of us are working. All of us are blessed with good families. And, all of us are faithful to God. The career that Mom chose blessed us more than we will ever know.

This world frequently judges people in terms of career advancement. By that, they mean money, status, power, and perks. We are wise to judge ourselves by a different standard (John 7:24). In God's economy, faithfulness equals success. All honest, moral work is honorable. Dignity lies in the effort, not in the status.

What is the answer to a "dead end" job? Perhaps there should be another question before there can be an answer. Perhaps we should ask ourselves, "Is this job helping me live faithfully before God?" Sometimes, it's better to change our thinking than it is to change our careers.

More and more people are discovering the fallacy of the success-at-all-cost career track. If you will pardon the adaptation of a statement from our Lord, they are realizing that one's life does not consist of the prominence of his career. One of my "old professors" taught me this truth many years ago. One day in a marriage and family class we asked him how he came to be in Auburn. His answer went something like this, "All our married life, my wife moved with me. She moved for graduate school. She moved for my doctoral studies. She moved for me to take a better job. She got a good job offer here, and I thought it was time that I moved for her." Our respect for him soared.

I call decisions like that pro-family decisions. It is very difficult to go wrong when we make such decisions. The money (or prominence) may be less, but the blessings will be greater. God will see to that!

WHAT CAN WE DO WHEN JOLTS COME?

As mentioned in the introduction, a frequent career jolt concerns age discrimination. Older workers, though not old, find themselves in the job market again. They did nothing wrong. It was just a matter of economics. Salaries and benefits tend to increase with tenure. After the merger, the company found it cheaper to keep only the younger workers. Years of loyal service seem to count for nothing.

We say, "seem to count for nothing." God knows.

God sees. God keeps count. The practice described above is lamentable. It may even be illegal. Sadly, it is also real. What can we do when such a jolt comes?

We can give ourselves permission to be angry. Unfairness should make us angry. Anger, in itself, is not a sin (Ephesians 4:26-27). We can give ourselves permission to be angry, but we dare not give ourselves permission to be bitter. Bitterness is such a damaging sin (Ephesians 4:31).

When career jolts come, we can give ourselves permission to grieve. Grief is not restricted to losses through death. One can grieve the loss of health, the loss of a friendship, and the loss of a job. Such grieving is not a sign of weak faith or poor mental health. It is a sign of humanity. If we are wise, we will grieve with those who grieve (Romans 12:15).

When career jolts come, we can turn to God in prayer. I know no better way to practice 1 Peter 5:6-7. Our lives are always in God's hands. Acts 17:28 begins, "For in Him we live and move and have our being ..." Scripture clearly teaches that the Lord takes care of His own (Matthew 6:25-34; Romans 8:31-39).

A career jolt may be the Lord's way of opening new doors in our lives. Most of us have experienced events that seemed so negative at the time. Years later, we find that our judgment has changed completely. The "negative" was actually a positive. It brought us nearer to God. It made us more grateful. It showed us who our friends really were. It helped us become more trusting and less self-sufficient.

When career jolts come, we can turn to brethren for help and support. Philippians 2:4 powerfully states, "Let each one of you look out not only for his own interests, but also for the interests of others." While spiritual interests come first, God leaves us free to help one another in countless ways.

The Lord's church is the Lord's family. "Brother" and "sister" are not religious titles. They are statements of divine fact. The Lord adds to the church those who are being saved (Acts 2:47). The Lord comforts His people so that we "can comfort others with the comfort which we ourselves are comforted by God" (2 Corinthians 1:3–4). This great passage applies to more than just the trouble which comes from persecution.

In our culture, men's unwillingness to ask for help seems legendary. We have been "sold a bill of goods" concerning the virtue of independence. True virtue lies in interdependence. We all need help at times. We are all blessed when we are given opportunity to help others. Family helping family is a win-win proposition. That is especially true within God's family.

When career jolts come, we can remember the lemonade. You know the lemonade theory: When life hands you lemons, use them to make lemonade. Ask yourself the following questions:

- What can I learn from this experience?
- How can God help me cope with this situation?
- Was I part of the cause of this career jolt? If so, how do I keep it from happening again?
- Has this jolt identified weaknesses in my life,

especially in my character or in my faith? If so, how can I begin to grow stronger?
- If there is some time between jobs, how can I use that time to the glory of God?

Please do not hear these words to be saying that the pain of career jolts is minor. It is anything but minor. At the same time, no pain is greater than God's ability to help us. The key to easing life's hurts—on any and every level—is to let God help.

CONCLUSION

My wife, Laura, and I are both teachers. I am blessed to teach in a Christian university. It's such a warm, positive, encouraging environment. As good as it is, I did not set out to become a teacher. My parents had to make me go to college. I would have been perfectly happy to have stayed on the farm. While in college, many good influences led to full time church work. After nearly twenty years of local ministry, what could be described as a career jolt put me in this teaching job.

What looked like a jolt was just a change. It was just a change because we were able to make it with God. I realize that we were "caught in a very soft net." Many better people have faced such difficult career reversals. Let us become part of their "net." Whenever we help bear any part of a brother's burden, we do "fulfill the law of Christ" (Galatians 6:2). What an honor to be able to help others in His name!

QUESTIONS FOR DISCUSSION

1. What has contributed to the seeming increase in career jolts faced by so many good people these days?
2. What is the danger in thinking of work in terms of "secular work" and "Christian work"?
3. Why does the Bible have such a high view of work?
4. In your judgment, do too many people base too much of their identity (their value, their worth, their self-image) on their careers?
5. Are career jolts inevitable? Give reasons for your answer.
6. Does God really care what kind of work we do? Explain.
7. Has this lesson overemphasized the ability of God to help us overcome job-related problems? Explain.

16

WHEN HURTS SHALL BE NO MORE

JACK P. WILHELM

We have not studied all of the things that can cause hurts in life, but we have studied enough to understand why the human family has always yearned for what is called Heaven. Sometimes the concept of heaven was not called by that term by all seekers, but there has been a universal longing to know what life beyond the grave offered.

Job, one of the first to put it in words, said, "If a man dies, shall he live again?" (Job 14:14) With Abraham, it may have been more just a continual searching as he moved from place to place and "waited for the city which has foundations, whose builder and maker is God" (Hebrews 11:10). David's hurt at the loss of his child was eased a bit when he resigned himself to the finality of his loss. He said, "Can I bring him back again? I shall go to him, but he shall not return to me" (2 Samuel 12:23).

UNBELIEVERS HAVE YEARNED TO KNOW

Even unbelievers have expressed a common yearning for comfort to ease the hurt of bereavement. In his classic sermon on "Our Eternal Home," Batsell Barrett Baxter referred to the poignant comments that Robert Ingersoll made in his "Eulogy at His Brother's Grave." Regarding Ingersoll, Baxter said:

> Mr. Ingersoll had the reputation of being an agnostic. He had no confidence in the Bible, Christianity, or the church. He had traveled about America time after time preaching against everything for which Christianity stands, especially the God of the Bible. He and his younger brother, Ralph, had entered into a pact that whichever one should die first, his funeral sermon would be preached by the one who lingered on. I suppose that Robert, the elder of the two brothers, expected that he would not be the one who should have to prepare a funeral sermon, but somehow it turned out otherwise. In the flowering manhood of middle life, the younger brother, Ralph, was taken, and it was Robert, the agnostic, who preached the funeral sermon. In Arlington Cemetery near Washington, D. C., Robert Ingersoll, the nation's most famous orator of his generation, stood and spoke of his yearning to know what lies beyond the grave. I want to quote a few lines of that speech. Somewhere near the middle, he says, "Life is a narrow vale between the cold and barren peaks of two

eternities. We strive in vain to look beyond the heights. We cry aloud, and the only answer is the echo of a wailing cry. From the voiceless lips of the unreplying dead there comes no word; but in the night of death, hope sees a star and listening, love can hear the rustle of a wing. He who sleeps here, when dying, mistaking the approach of death for the return of health, whispered with his latest breath, 'I am better now.' Let us believe in spite of doubts and dogmas and tears and fears that these dear words are true of all the countless dead'." (Sermon preached by Batsell Barrett Baxter, September 23, 1956 at Hillsboro church in Nashville, TN.)

We have always heard that "there are no atheists in foxholes." They, and folks like Ingersoll, and most others who honestly face eternity want to believe that Heaven really exists and will be the place where hurts shall be no more. It is said that when Phillips Brooks was near death, he was so ill he could not see even any of his close religious friends. Robert Ingersoll was passing through and, upon inquiry, was permitted to see Brooks. Ingersoll said, "I don't know what to make of this—your seeing me when you've not been seeing any of your close church friends?"

Brooks replied, "I hope to see all of them again in heaven, but this may be my last chance to see you!"

Even the careless and irreverent seem to think more soberly when the reality of death confronts them. We've all smiled about the story of W. C. Fields who was reading through the Bible near the end of his life, a stance somewhat out of character to the image he had always portrayed. When asked why, he said, "Looking for loopholes."

It is said that when Humphrey Bogart died, Lauren Bacall placed a gold whistle in his coffin with him and said, "If you need anything, just whistle," a memorable line from one of the movies they had done together.

We should not wait too late to learn more about heaven and how to go there. But we will still want to know more than we are told, even in the Bible.

WHY IS OUR KNOWLEDGE OF HEAVEN SO LIMITED?

We often speak of "displaced persons," meaning that some are homeless and have no permanent lodging. That will not be so in Eternity, because two places are being prepared and everyone will be in one of them. Jesus said, "I go to prepare a place for you" (John 14:1–3). In it, there will be no troubled hearts and hurts. He also spoke of a place "prepared for the devil and his angels" (Matthew 25:41–46). Everything we learn about heaven causes us to want to go there. Everything we learn about hell repulses us and motivates us to miss it by all means.

I once told my wife's principal in Auburn that I wondered, if one was unfortunate enough to go to the bad place, if part of the punishment might be having to sit through 1,000 years of pointless, plotless, tear jerker movies or miniseries as often shown on TV, followed by a 1,000 years of girls' basketball back when it was played so delicately and slowly with the half court restrictions

—and all that time with nothing to eat but oat bran! He said, "If I really had reason to believe that's what it would be like, it would be enough to get me to change my ways!" Regarding torment, I think we can safely say it will be worse even than that.

But what about heaven? We are not told as much as we would like to know. Are there any possible ways to understand why?

Is it because we walk by faith and not by sight? (2 Corinthians 5:7). We know enough here to avoid troubled hearts and look forward to the time when we will know more (John 14:1–6; 1 John 3:2).

Is it because we might get distracted? If we knew more, we might neglect doing the less thrilling duties that prepare us. In 2 Corinthians 12:1–9, the one caught up "into Paradise ... heard inexpressible words, which it is not lawful for a man to utter." Some have observed that God has never intended us to be in but one world at a time. When Lazarus came back from the dead (John 11,12), there is no indication that he went on the lecture circuit to discuss details about the other world. Perhaps it was "not lawful" and he was restricted.

Is it because of our own inability to comprehend? I preached for 10 years for a congregation where there were probably 10 to 15 PhDs in the audience every Sunday. They were experts in their fields, including several fields of civil, chemical and electrical engineering, parasitology, veterinary medicine, mathematics, aerospace, languages, advanced computer technology, and others. No one ever suggested that we get those PhDs to give our pre-school toddlers a head start by teaching those subjects to them. Was it because the PhDs did not know their subjects? Of course, they were capable and knowledgeable, but the toddlers could not have comprehended what they were saying because of their own limited vocabularies. Heaven deals with eternal concepts. We are limited to temporal concepts. We cannot talk very long about eternity without contradicting ourselves. We speak of the "ceaseless ages," and "where will you spend eternity?" An age is limited, thus not ceaseless. Eternity is never ending, therefore cannot be spent.

WHAT IS HEAVEN LIKE?

God has accommodated us in our limitations. He uses things we are familiar with to give us an insight. A preacher once illustrated that approach by telling of the rancher who had never been away from his ranch until he made a trip to New York. When he returned, his children eagerly wanted to hear what the big city was like. He compared the skyscrapers to the silo and the subways to mole tunnels in the yard. He did not mean that they were identical, but they were the closest things he could use that they were familiar with.

Sometimes figurative language is used in the Bible, and we have trouble if we try to make it all literal. G. C. Brewer told once of a man who got disenchanted about heaven. He had read Revelation 21:16 and learned that "the city is laid out as a square, and its length is as great as its breadth. And he measured the city with the reed:

twelve thousand furlongs. Its length, breadth, and height are equal."

With mind boggling calculations, the man had computed how much space a soul would require in heaven and decided that a squared area of only 12,000 furlongs in width by 12,000 furlongs in breadth was not going to be room enough for all the saved! Being disillusioned, he was about ready to give up his faith. Realizing that it would be futile to try to answer such technical tidbits on their own merits, Brewer simply said, "Aren't you overlooking something? The last part of that verse mentions that it is 12,000 furlongs high as well as long and wide." The man was elated when he realized it would be a cube, not a square area. He said, "I hadn't thought of that! It says its length, breadth, and height are equal! That way, we can get the whole human family in!" We may have real problems if we do not let figurative language be figurative language, but at least it can still create an appeal in our hearts to go to heaven.

FIGURES USED IN THE BIBLE

A few of those figures used in the Bible make heaven more understandable and appealing to us:

- It is as a new dwelling with beauty and security in contrast to the tent dwellings ancients knew (2 Corinthians 4, 5). As it turns out, we are all "tent dwellers," either content or discontent. Fortunately, we can decide

which one we want to be, regardless of the other circumstances about us.
- It is as a new body versus the decayed, weakening bodies we have here (1 Corinthians 15).
- It is as a bride's wedding day (Revelation 21:2).
- It is as a beautiful walled city with many jewels and a street paved with gold (Revelation 21:10ff).
- It is as a homecoming and reunion (Matthew 8:11ff; Luke 13:29ff).
- It is as a state of deliverance and immunity from evil and wicked tyrants (Matthew 8:12; Revelation 21:8).

If you will picture the mindset and the living conditions of the ancient readers of this information when it was first given, you can see how appealing the hope would be to them to be liberated from the hurts that they confronted almost daily.

OTHER PICTURES OF HEAVEN

Heaven is pictured as a place of rest. Perhaps a lazy, flabby, and spoiled society whose main activity of each day is to watch the sun travel from east to west would care little for this, but for most of us, rest is appealing. Hebrews 3 and 4 speak of the rest that remains for the people of God, and Revelation 14:13 especially puts it in focus: "Blessed are the dead who die in the Lord from now on that they may rest from their labors, and their works follow them."

A part of the hurts of life involves toiling and laboring continuously. Solomon said,

> I hated life because the work that was done under the sun was grievous to me, for all is vanity and grasping for the wind ... For all his days are sorrowful, and his work grievous; even in the night his heart takes no rest. This also is vanity (Ecclesiastes 2:17, 23).

Heaven is pictured as a place of joyful activity. To some who are part of a lively generation, heaven might seem boring. A teen once said, "If heaven is going to be like church, I'm not sure I want to go!" Don't let the fact that it is a place of rest and serenity fool you. It will not be boring to those who actually go, because they will have cultivated on earth a joyful appreciation and spiritual interests in order to go. With service to God and beautiful singing, there will be abundant activity: "Therefore they are before the throne of God and serve him day and night in his temple. And he who sits on the throne shall dwell among them" (Revelation 7:15). Revelation 15:3 adds to that: "They sing the song of Moses, the servant of God, and the song of the Lamb." In addition to the old song of Moses, "they sang as if were a new song before the throne" (Revelation 14:3). That should please those who want a balance in old songs and new songs!

Heaven is pictured as a place where all sorrows and hurts of life will be absent. It truly will be the place where hurts shall be no more! "And God will wipe away every tear from their eyes; there shall be no more death nor sorrow nor crying; and there shall be no more pain, for the former things have passed away" (Revelation 21:4). He adds that all things will be new. We are assured also that death will be banished (1 Corinthians 15:26, 54–57; Revelation 20:14).

The ancient Bible characters knew the hurts of hunger, thirst, and burning heat. In heaven, "They shall neither hunger anymore nor thirst anymore; the sun shall not strike them, nor any heat ... the Lamb ... will shepherd them and lead them to living fountains of waters. And God will wipe away every tear from their eyes" (Revelation 7:16–17). With all of our creature comforts, we may find it difficult to comprehend how much these assurances meant to the first readers of Revelation, but other hurts we do experience should help us find a good measure of interest in going to such a place.

A man wondered if he had a "near death" experience because of a weird remembrance he had after being put to sleep. He was asked some questions about it. He said, "I first thought perhaps I had died and sensed that I was hungry, and my feet were cold. But the more I thought about it, I realize that it had to be only a hallucination. I could not have died, because if I was in heaven, I would not have been hungry and if I was not in heaven, my feet would not have been cold!"

Heaven is pictured as a place that is holy and peaceful. It seems that every generation has had its mad men to contend with. Many nations and families have known only bickering, war, and uncertainty for generations. We see on the TV news the pitiful, helpless children who stare in bewilderment. Many have been abandoned or left as orphans by acts of violence. Fear must grip their little bodies and minds in ways we cannot imagine. Even adults especially the aged, walk with aimless feet as they are shown on occasional news reports. That is sad, but there are also times when good Christian people suffer when the peace of a congregation is shattered. It has often been said that nothing is nastier than a church fuss! It will help if Christians will remember that the sin condemned most frequently and severely in the Bible is the sin of division among God's people!

To those who know these hurts, whatever the cause, some scriptures may be especially comforting as we anticipate heaven, the place where hurts shall be no more:

- Revelation 21:8: "the cowardly, unbelieving, abominable, murderers, sexually immoral, sorcerers, idolaters, and all liars shall have their part in the lake which burns with fire and brimstone, which is the second death."
- Revelation 21:27: "But there shall by no means enter it anything that defiles, or causes and abomination or a lie, but only those who are written in the Lamb's Book of Life."
- Hebrews 12:14: "Pursue peace with all men, and holiness, without which no one will see the Lord."

Heaven is pictured as a place where all our curiosities can be satisfied. Here there are still many things we do not know and curiosities that God has not fully revealed. Every preacher at some time has been so grateful that God gave us Deuteronomy 29:29, that "the secret things belong to God." So when people ask us those questions that make angels stagger, we can say God has not told us that, so we will have to be content to leave that with him, even as the arch angel once left it up to God to settle a dispute (Jude 9). Of course, it is better if we can truthfully say, "The Bible does not say; therefore, I don't know," than merely to have to say, "I don't know" because of ignorance.

There are some curiosities that are quite normal that we may wonder about. At times when people ask about them, we simply have to say, "We don't know. Here is a scripture that might help, or here is another thought that might help, but someday we will have the benefit of further knowledge." 1 John 3:2 is a helpful verse to assure us of that:

> Beloved, now we are children of God; and it has not yet been revealed what we shall be, but we know that when he is revealed, we shall be like him, for we shall see him as he is.

Our "whys" cry out for answers; our limitations underscore our helplessness—and sometimes become the basis for "digs" the world thrusts at believers. The world likes to say, "IF there is a God, why does he allow pain and evil? If he can't prevent it, he doesn't qualify to be God. If he has the power to prevent it and won't, then he doesn't qualify to be a loving God." We would all like some neat, convincing answers, yet not even the church itself is free of things that puzzle. [Check pages 1-7 of my book *Contemporary Concerns of Christians* for a discussion of pain, evil, and atrocities of the Old Testament.]

Many curiosities abound about death and the afterlife. The following scriptures may help as we look forward to a time when our curiosities will be made clear:

- 1 Corinthians 13:12: "For now we see in a mirror, dimly; but then face to face. Now I know in part, but then I shall know as I also am known."
- Romans 8:18: " ... the sufferings of this present time are not worthy to be compared with the glory which shall be revealed in us."
- 2 Corinthians 4:17-18: "our light affliction which is but for a moment, is working for us a far more exceeding and eternal weight of glory ... while we do not look at the things which are not seen. For the things which are seen are temporary, but the things which are not seen are eternal."
- Philippians 3:20-21:"For our citizenship is in heaven, from which we also eagerly wait for the Savior, the Lord Jesus Christ, who will transform our lowly body that it may be conformed to his glorious body, according to

the working by which he is able even to subdue all things to himself." [Therefore, "stand fast" 4:1.]

QUESTIONS THAT ARISE

When we speak of heaven as the place where hurts will be no more, several questions arise which are not really a part of the scope of this study: We have curiosities about what happens when we die, are we conscious after death, do we have the same identities, will we know each other, do those on the other side see us as we go about our daily activities, is belief in reincarnation defensible, will there be degrees of reward and punishment, are near death experiences real, do we need a living will, and many more.

One question emerges that concerns some people that does fall in the scope of this study. People wonder how they can be free of hurt and happy in heaven if they know pain is taking place in hell at the same time—and especially if they realize that their loved ones are not with them in heaven.

One thought that may help is to realize that we can be happy here, in this life even though pain and hurt are taking place all around us. Most of us would not have to go more than a block from our homes to find people who are hurting, yet we are relatively insensitive to it. There are times when our lives have been filled with laughter and joy even though the news daily shows us much turmoil and war-torn strife going on not far from our shores. We are not glad that is the case. We just know it happens, even in an imperfect world. In Heaven there will be a perfection and beauty which will be more absorbing of our interest and attention than anything in this life.

Add to that thought the realization that God will let heaven be heaven for us. Perhaps like the Sadducees, we do err "not knowing the power of God" (Matthew 22:29). The Bible teaches us that "God will wipe away every tear from their eyes; there shall be no more death, nor sorrow, nor crying; and there shall be no more pain, for the former things have passed away" (Revelation 21:4).

We do not like to think of pain. We do not like to think of death. Jim Bill McInteer said, "I'm not afraid of death—but I would just rather not be there when it happens!" Unfortunately, we do not have a choice. But we can be comforted in knowing that God has great things in store for the successful believer who overcomes. Heaven, the place where hurts shall be no more, will be worth it all.

There is a poem by Tom Holland that I would like to use to close this chapter. When I called Tom to ask for his permission to include it, he not only graciously granted permission, but he asked if I would like to know the background that prompted his writing the poem. I was very interested in knowing how it came about.

There was a good lady in the congregation where he preached who had suffered many hurts. Her son had fought a very draining battle and had been very sick with Hodgkin disease before it went into remission. Soon her husband had a heart attack and died suddenly. Before long, she got the shattering news that led to a mastectomy. As Tom was en route to the hospital at the time of her surgery, he was praying desperately for some wisdom and insight as to what he could possibly say to one who had been through so much.

When he entered her room, he told her, "I want to ask you a question-and I will respect your right not to answer it."

She said, "What is it?"

He said, "Have you ever found yourself asking 'Why?'" She replied, "I certainly have! Over and over!"

He said, "Then I think it is time for you to change questions. Instead of 'Why' you need to begin asking 'What'."

To bring that thought to full fruition, Tom then went to his office and wrote the following poem which he shared with her. Sometime later, he spoke for her memorial service. Prior to her death, she told him that the poem had a significant impact on her life. If you are having heavy burdens that prompt your asking "Why," maybe you can find the poem to be of some help also in easing life's hurts.

Changing Questions
by Tom Holland

God's suffering people may often ask "Why"
Must the heartache, pain and care
Sweep down upon them in merciless waves
And cast them down to despair.

God's faithful children sighing and dying.

Where is God when the body is caught
In the clutches of excruciating pain?
Is there a reason? Are lessons to be taught?

To know the "whys" would perhaps give
  strength; There would seem to be no control.
But great men of God have searched for the
  "why"—The quest started in long days
  of old.

Maybe it is time to ponder again,
The death, the suffering and pain.
Only now let us look from a different view,
Not limited by a life so mundane.

We may never really know the "why" of it now.
But one thing we can understand,
The "what" we will do in the face of it all,
Determined to follow God's plan.

What shall we do to show in our pain
The love of our God for us still?
What shall we do in the face of sure death God's
  gracious will to fulfill?

We shall glorify the Loving God of all grace,
We shall never denounce or deride.
We shall love Him in sunshine and in the rain
'Till we in heaven are safe by His side.

QUESTIONS FOR DISCUSSION

1. How do you explain what appears to be a universal yearning in the hearts of people from the beginning of time for assurance that there will be life after death?
2. Have you personally known anyone who was an unbeliever without any fear of life beyond the grave? If they have already died, was there any indication of concern or apprehension as they approached the end?
3. Discuss the possibilities as to why we have not been told more about heaven. Are there other possibilities you might add to those listed?
4. Elaborate on some of the figures which have been used to help us understand heaven better. What comes to your mind when you think of some of them, e.g. a new dwelling, a new body, the bride's wedding day, a walled city, a homecoming and reunion, and freedom from despots?
5. What would you say to a youth who made a statement as the one quoted: "If heaven is going to be like church, I'm not sure I want to go"? What might congregations and those who plan worship services think about if that sentiment is widespread?
6. Do you know anyone who claims to have had a "near death" experience? Are there

explanations as to what happened that would call their validity into question?
7. Have you had some of the curiosities mentioned that you look forward to getting more information about? Have you had other curiosities than those mentioned?

SCRIPTURE INDEX

Old Testament		16:6–16	149	39	188
Genesis		18:16–19	22	39:9	30
1–2	118	18:19	153	45	95
1:26	20	20:11	84	50	95
1:26–27	98, 178	21	2, 121	**Leviticus**	
1:31	107	21:8–21	149	19:16	8, 28
2:15	186	22	153	19:18	19
2:18	107	24	188	20:1–6	1
2:19–20	186	25:28	121, 150	**Deuteronomy**	
2:24	115, 150	26:7	84	4	156
3:12	121	26:22	2	4:9–14	155
3:16	107	29–30	122	6	156, 158
3:17–19	107, 186	29:15–30:13	150	6:1–9	155
3:22–24	107	29:20	75	6:4–9	153, 158
4	149	31–33	153	8:18	162
4:1–16	107	32:8	154	28:43	167
6:8	22	32:9–12	154	28:47	167
9:18–29	149	32:13–21	154	29:29	207
12:13	84	33	95	32:35	99
13	175	33:4	154	**Joshua**	
14:21–24	174	37	3	1:1–9	40
16	121, 149	37:24	150	7	175

215

SCRIPTURE INDEX

Judges
2:7–10	155
6:11–16	40
14	122

Ruth
1:15–18	75

1 Samuel
1	122
1–4	160
2	150
2:22–25	150
3:13	145, 150
8:1–5	160
16:7	5, 101
17:37	45
18:9	8
19:1	45
20:30–34	45
23:16	45
25	167
30:6	44

2 Samuel
11–12	84
12:23	196
13–14	71
13:21	150
14:33	71
15:1	16
18:5	71, 152
18:32	152
18:33	71, 152

1 Kings
3:1–15	174
11	122
11:1–13	146

2 Kings
5:20–27	175

1 Chronicles
28:9ff	146

2 Chronicles
7:17ff	146

Esther
1	122
6:7–9	16

Job
14:14	196
42:9–10	31
42:12	174

Psalms
8:5	20
10:4	15
26:5	81
37	85, 86, 88, 91
37:1	81, 84
37:3	88
37:4	87
37:5	90
37:7	86
37:7–8	92
37:9	81
37:9–10	92
37:12–13	86
37:17–18	86
37:23–24	86
37:34	92
46	76
58:1–6	83
73	85
73:2	85
73:16	86
73:16–19	85
78:1–7	83
94:16	81
119:115	81
127:3	1
127:3–5	131
139:14	20

Proverbs
3:34	9, 15
6:6–11	180
6:17	9
9:18	157
10:4–5	180
11:13	8, 28
11:24–26	180
11:28	168
13:24	152, 157
14:12	17
14:29	62
14:31	179
15:1–4	8
16:18	15
16:32	123
17:10	157
17:22	10
18:8	29
18:24	8, 46
19:18	152
20:1	123
20:19	8, 29
21:2	17
22:1	123
22:6	141, 142, 143, 145, 146
22:15	157, 158
22:28	143
23:4–5	123, 177
23:6–8	176
23:13–14	152, 157
23:23	41
23:29–35	123
24:19–22	85
24:30–34	123, 180

SCRIPTURE INDEX

25:23	8	5:13–16	20, 31	25:21	43
25:27	16	5:16	44	25:23	43
26:20	29	5:38–48	100	25:34	13
26:20–22	8	5:44	98	25:27	171
26:22	29	6:1–4	xii, 183	25:41–46	199
27	42	6:1–5	42	27:1–10	23
27:2	16	6:12	96	**Mark**	
29:15	152, 157	6:13–14	96	1:9–11	24
29:25	84	6:14–15	8, 96	2:23–28	35
30:7–9	165, 179	6:16–18	42	6:31	19
31	129, 156, 186	6:19–21	168	9:22	87
Ecclesiastes		6:25–34	192	10:21	71
2:17	204	7:12	11, 19, 47, 100	12:37	177
2:23	204			12:41	183
2:24	186	7:13–14	72	14:3–9	170
5:10–11	123, 177	8:11ff	203	**Luke**	
5:10–13	166	8:12	203	5:31–32	34
8:11–13	84	8:19	22	6:20	180
Isaiah		9:11	34	6:26	48
1:7–9	180	9:21	22	7:22	179
5:1–7	71	10:16	90	7:36–50	34
40:27–31	76	10:28	84	9:25	177
53:3	2, 24	10:39	88	12	54, 168
56:11	167	12:49–50	22	12:15	161, 178
Jeremiah		13:22	168	13:3–5	31
10:23	17	13:54–57	34	13:29ff	203
31:34	102	15:28	22	14:7–11	16
Ezekiel		18:15	100	14:11	16
18	154	18:15–17	99, 101	14:12–14	56
Daniel		18:21–35	97	15:11–32	74, 95
4:28–37	16	18:22	101	15:13	169
6	188	19:3–9	108, 118	15:30	169
New Testament		19:5	115	16:9	173
Matthew		20:25–28	90	16:11	168
1:11	22	22:29	210	16:19–31	23, 176
1:18–25	122	22:34–40	183	17:1	35
5:10–12	35	22:39	19	17:3–4	8, 100, 101
5:11	36	23:37	75, 79	17:5–10	44

217

SCRIPTURE INDEX

Reference	Page	Reference	Page	Reference	Page
18:9–11	9	5:23–30	36	12:15	192
18:18–23	23	5:29	94	12:16	16
18:24–25	177	5:41	24	12:18	145
19:28–40	23	7:60	95, 100	12:19	99
20:45–47	16	8–9	91	12:19–21	96
22:13–25	23	9:13	83	12:21	187
23:34	95, 96, 100	9:15	188	13	13
23:39–43	12	10:34–35	12	13:1–7	130
John		10:38	88	14:15–21	31
1:11	2	12:20–24	48	16:1–12	22
1:29	72	13:22	16	**1 Corinthians**	
1:46	34	13:44–45	36	1:4–8	11
3:16	20, 55	16:1–5	155	1:4–9	40
6:51	72	16:25	45	4:17–21	37
7:24	190	17:11	22	6:9–11	12
8	119	17:28	19, 192	6:11	119
8:29	36	18:1–3	188	7:1–5	112
8:44	123	18:24–28	33	8:9–13	31
10:10	21	20:25	21	9	42
10:11	72	20:34	188	9:1–23	37
11–12	200	20:35	183	10:13	35
12:42–43	47	**Romans**		10:32	31
14	40	1:8	22, 40	12:12–31	20
14:1–3	199	1:30	8	13	30, 57, 58, 75, 77
14:1–4	44	3:1–8	37	13:1–3	58, 178
14:1–6	200	3:9–18	17	13:4a	58
14:6	41	3:23	17, 95	13:4b	59
14:27	21	5:3–4	xi	13:4c	59
15:12–13	55	5:6–11	17, 75, 98, 100	13:4d	59
16:1–3	35			13:4e	60
17:17	129	5:8	20, 55	13:4–7	8
18:15–18	84	8:18	208	13:5a	61
Acts		8:28	91	13:5b	62
1:15–20	23	8:31–39	192	13:5c	62
2:36–38	12	9:1–5	72	13:5d	63
2:36–40	90	12	13	13:6a	63
2:47	193	12:3	16, 18	13:6b	64
5:1–11	175	12:9–21	75, 77		

SCRIPTURE INDEX

13:7a	64	6:1	32	2:1–11	77
13:7b	65	6:1–2	101	2:3	9
13:7c	65	6:1–5	24	2:3–4	19
13:7d	66	6:2	194	2:4	192
13:8	69	6:3	9, 16	2:5–11	24, 90
13:8a	66	6:4	19	2:12	10
13:8ff	142	6:7	46	2:12–13	19, 104
13:11	158	6:7–10	104	3:19–30	22
13:12	208	6:9	43	3:20–21	208
15	203	6:10	89	4:1	209
15:10	9	**Ephesians**		4:6–7	21
15:26	205	2:1–10	12, 17	4:11	165
15:33	142, 144	2:8–10	9	4:14–19	12
15:54–57	205	2:10	43	**Colossians**	
15:57–58	21	4:11–16	20, 158	1:3–8	11, 22
16:15–18	22	4:25	41, 123	3:1–2	88
2 Corinthians		4:26–27	192	3:7–15	22
1:3–4	193	4:26–32	101	3:12–13	8
3:1–2	37	4:28	123	3:13	96
4–5	202	4:29–32	9, 123	3:20–21	131
4:17–18	208	4:31	192	3:21	144, 158
5:7	200	4:31–32	8	3:22–24	187
7:8–12	24	4:32	96, 97	3:23–24	43
8:1–5	11–12	5	65, 118, 130	4:2	20
8:1–7	183	5:1	96	4:6	9
8:18–21	10	5:21	131	**1 Thessalonians**	
8:20–23	37	5:22–24	130, 131	1:2–5	11
9:7	183	5:22–33	125, 129	1:2–10	22
10:8–18	37	5:25–30	131	1:9	33
11:5–31	37	5:28–29	19	2:1–12	188
12:1–9	200	5:31	115	2:13	33
12:11–21	42, 188	5:33	131	4:9–10	77
Galatians		6:1–4	32, 131, 156	**2 Thessalonians**	
2:11	32, 33	6:4	144, 153	1:3–8	11
5:13–17	31	6:21	22	3:1–2	9
5:19–21	183	**Philippians**		3:1–3	36
5:19–23	8	1:3–6	11	3:4	10
5:22	21	1:12ff	91	3:6–10	188

219

SCRIPTURE INDEX

1 Timothy		5:8–9	34	2:23–24	38
1:12–17	9	5:12–14	88	3:1–6	76, 131
1:15–17	12	8:12	102	3:7	112, 131
2:12–15	107	10:24	21	3:8	61
4:1–5	48	11:8–16	153	3:9	35
5:8	118, 189	11:10	196	3:15–16	37
5:13	29	11:13–16	24	3:16	36, 81
6:3–10	177	12:14	206	4:12–19	24
6:3–19	123	13:1	68	4:15	81
6:3–21	175	13:4	107, 118	5:5	9, 15, 131
6:5	175	13:17	131	5:5–7	189
6:6–8	176	**James**		5:6–7	192
6:7	168, 176	1:2–3	10	**1 John**	
6:9	168, 175, 176	1:13	105	3:2	200, 207
6:9–10	175, 176	1:17	129	3:16	55
6:9–11	161	1:19–20	62	4:9	55
6:10	172, 175	1:27	89	4:10	55
6:17	168, 176	2	181	4:11	55
6:18–19	176	2:1–9	9, 13	**3 John**	
2 Timothy		2:1–13	180	2	162
1:3–5	154	2:3b	181	9–10	23
2:3–7	35	2:6–7	183	9–11	9
2:23	13	2:9	180	**Jude**	
2:23–25	9	2:14–26	47	9	207
3:1–5	19	3	9	**Revelation**	
3:14–15	154	3:1ff	8	4	86–87
3:14–17	129	3:14–18	36, 59	7:15	204
Titus		4:6	15	7:16–17	205
1:10–16	29	5	171	14:3	204
2:1–8	129	5:1	171	14:13	203
2:1–10	155	5:1–3	171	15:3	204
2:9–10	187	5:11	31	20:14	205
2:14	43	**1 Peter**		21:2	203
3:1–2	130	2:11–12	24	21:4	24, 205, 210
Hebrews		2:12	81, 88	21:8	203, 206
3	203	2:14	81	21:10ff	203
4	203	2:18–25	130	21:16	201
4:15	95	2:19–20	38	21:27	206

CPSIA information can be obtained
at www.ICGtesting.com
Printed in the USA
JSHW011018270920
8263JS00005B/18